Practical Ideas
That Really Work
for Students with ADHD

Second Edition

Grade 5 Through Grade 12

Kathleen McConnell

Gail R. Ryser

pro·ed
An International Publisher

8700 Shoal Creek Boulevard
Austin, Texas 78757-6897
800/897-3202   Fax 800/397-7633
www.proedinc.com

© 2000, 2005 by PRO-ED, Inc.
8700 Shoal Creek Boulevard
Austin, Texas 78757-6897
800/897-3202   Fax 800/397-7633
www.proedinc.com

Printed in the United States of America

1   2   3   4   5   6   7   8   9   10   08   07   06   05   04

Contents

Introduction

We created *Practical Ideas That Really Work for Students with ADHD* for educators who work with students who have attention, impulsivity, or hyperactivity problems that interfere with their ability to learn. The materials are intended for use with students in preschool through Grade 12 and include two main components:

- **Evaluation form with a rating scale and ideas matrix.** The rating scale portion of the evaluation form is a criterion-referenced measure for evaluating behaviors that affect student learning. The items on the scale are specific descriptors that are correlated to the *Diagnostic and Statistical Manual of Mental Disorders–Fourth Edition–Text Revision* (DSM–IV–TR) indicators for ADHD. The ideas matrix on the evaluation form provides a systematic way of linking the results of the rating scale to interventions. We hope that educators use the matrix as a tool for selecting effective interventions to meet each student's specific needs.

- **Resource manual.** The practical ideas were written to assist teachers and other professionals in improving students' attending and organization skills and decreasing their behavior problems related to impulsivity and hyperactivity. The book contains a one-page explanation of each idea, along with reproducible worksheets, examples, illustrations, and tips designed for easy implementation.

The materials in this book are intended for use with students in Grades 5 through 12. A second book of practical ideas for younger students with ADHD is available in this series and is intended for use with students in preschool through Grade 4. The general approaches and philosophy in the two books are the same; however, the forms that accompany the practical ideas in the version for younger students include many pictures and require little reading ability. The forms in this version for older students are more sophisticated and require some reading. Teachers of students in Grades 4 or 5 may want to examine both volumes and select the book that best fits the maturity and reading level of their students.

The next section of this introduction will describe the development of the rating scale and the ideas, then provide directions for their use.

The Rating Scale

The criterion-referenced rating scale is intended for use by teachers or other professionals to rate students according to the DSM–IV–TR criteria for ADHD. The measure was designed to assist teachers in conducting a careful and thorough assessment of the specific problems to guide the selection of intervention strategies.

The rating scale is divided into the three areas of ADHD defined by the DSM–IV–TR: inattention, hyperactivity, and impulsivity. The measure consists of 54 items—three items for each of the 18 DSM–IV–TR criteria. Educators can use the scale's 4-point Likert scale to complete a rating, with a 0 meaning the student never exhibits the behavior and a 3 meaning the student consistently exhibits the behavior to the point where it almost always interferes with the child's ability to function in the learning environment. For each DSM–IV–TR criterion, the range of possible scores is 0 to 9; the higher the score, the more the behavior interferes with learning.

The criterion-referenced measure was field-tested in three school districts in Texas with 84 students identified as having ADHD. The students ranged in age from 6 to 16, with 17 females and 67 males. An item analysis was conducted using this sample and the resulting reliability coefficients were .97 for inattention, .96 for hyperactivity, and .96 for impulsivity. The magnitude of these coefficients strongly suggests that the rating scale possesses little test error and that users can have confidence in its results.

One way of establishing an assessment instrument's validity is to study the performance of different groups of individuals on the instrument. Each group's results should make sense, given what is known about the relationship of the instrument's content to the group. In the case of our rating scale, one would expect that individuals identified as having ADHD would be rated higher by their teachers or other professionals than individuals not so identified. In fact, an instrument whose results did not differentiate between such groups would have no clinical or diagnostic value; it would have no construct validity.

We would expect to find statistically significant differences between individuals identified as having ADHD and those individuals identified as not having ADHD. To test for the differences, three *t* tests were conducted (one for each of the three areas of ADHD related to the DSM–IV–TR) with 84 students identified as having ADHD and 22 students with no known disabilities. The Bonferroni procedure was used to control for Type I error and alpha was set at 0.017. In every case, the group with ADHD was rated higher (i.e., had more difficulty functioning in the learning environment) than the group with no known disabilities. On the inattention total score, the ADHD group had a mean raw score of 58.7 (out of a possible score of 81), with a standard deviation of 17.5. For the no-disability group, the mean was 21.7 and the standard deviation was 15.4. On the hyperactivity total score, the ADHD group had a mean raw score of 31.5 (out of a possible score of 54), with a standard deviation of 15.3. For the no-disability group, the mean was 9.5 and the standard deviation was 10.4. On the inattention total score, the ADHD group had a mean raw score of 16.7 (out of a possible score of 27), with a standard deviation of 8.1. For the no-disability group, the mean was 3.9 and the standard deviation was 16.0. In each comparison, there were statistically significant differences between the mean raw scores of the two groups at the .000 level.

Practical Ideas That Really Work

Teachers and other educators are busy people with many responsibilities. In our discussions with teachers, supervisors, and counselors about the development of this product, they consistently emphasized the need for materials that are practical, easy to implement in the classroom, and not overly time consuming. We appreciated their input and worked hard to meet their criteria as we developed the ideas in this book. In addition, we conducted an extensive review of the literature, so that we stayed focused on ideas supported by data documenting their effectiveness. The result is a book with 37 ideas, most with reproducible masters, and all grounded in our research and collective experiences, as well as the many educators who advised us and shared information with us.

Assessment often provides much useful information about the strengths and deficits of students. However, unless the information gathered during the assessment process impacts instruction, its usefulness for campus-based educators is limited. We designed the ideas matrix so that educators can make the direct link between the information provided by the rating scale and instruction in the classroom. We believe that this format stays true to our purpose of presenting information that is practical and useful.

Directions for Using the Materials

The professional (a general education teacher, special education teacher, counselor, or other educator with knowledge of the student) should begin by completing the ADHD Evaluation Form for the student who has been identified as having ADHD or a student who exhibits problems with inattention, hyperactivity, or impulsivity. As an example, a completed Evaluation Form for a student, Kelly, is provided at the end of this section (see Figure 1). Space is provided on the front of the form for pertinent information about the student being rated, including name, birth date, age, school, grade, rater, and subject area. In addition, the dates the student is observed and the amount of time the rater spends with the student can be recorded here. Also included on the front of the form are the DSM–IV–TR criteria for attention-deficit/hyperactivity disorder.

Pages 2 and 3 of the ADHD Evaluation Form contain the rating scale. The items are divided into the three sections defined by the DSM–IV–TR criteria: inattention, hyperactivity, and impulsivity. This section provides the instructions for administering and scoring the items. Space is also provided to total the items for each DSM–IV–TR criterion, to check the three problems to target for immediate intervention, and to record the intervention idea and its starting date.

The last page of the Evaluation Form contains the ideas matrix. After choosing the three priority problems to target for immediate intervention, the professional should turn to the ideas matrix and select an intervention that corresponds to that problem. The professional should write the idea number and the starting date on the space provided on the rating scale.

For example, Kelly received the highest ratings in two areas of Inattention (incomplete assignments [9] and unorganized [7]) and one area of Impulsivity (speaks without permission [6]). Her teacher has targeted these three areas and has chosen Ideas 5, 6, 23, and 24 from the ideas matrix. Because the area of major concern is incomplete assignments, the teacher will begin with Idea 24 on October 4.

After selecting an idea from the matrix, the teacher can read the one-page explanation, then begin implementing the idea. To aid in implementation, most of the 37 ideas have at least one reproducible form on the page(s) immediately following the explanation. Some ideas did not lend themselves to a reproducible form, but instead are supported with explanations, suggestions for use, illustrations, tips, resource lists, and boxes of further information.

Ideally, the teacher or other professional should evaluate the effectiveness of each intervention. In our example with Kelly, this could be accomplished by recording the number of completed assignments during a 3- to 4-week period. If the intervention is successful, the teacher can move on to the second problem and choose a new idea to implement.

Research Supporting the Practical Ideas

The next section provides references that support the practical ideas in the book. These references will provide interested professionals with relevant information should they wish to learn more about the interventions. The references are grouped by general category.

The Importance of the Classroom Environment

Carbone, E. (2001). Arranging the classroom with an eye (and ear) to students with ADHD. *Teaching Exceptional Children, 34*(2), 72–81.

Christian, J. M. (1997). The body as a site of reproduction and resistance: Attention deficit hyperactivity disorder and the classroom. *Interchange, 28*(1) 31–43.

Overton, T. (2004). Promoting academic success through environmental assessment. *Intervention in School and Clinic, 39*(3), 147–153.

Sulzer-Azaroff, B., & Mayer, G. R. (1991). *Behavior analysis for lasting change.* Fort Worth, TX: Holt, Rinehart & Winston.

Helping Students Get Organized

Rief, S. F. (1996). Making a difference in the classroom. *The ADHD Report, 4*(2), 9–10.

Robin, A. L. (2001) Gee whiz, I missed it again: Improving time management skills. *Attention, 7*(5), 7–11.

Sewell Finkel, J. (2000) Living and succeeding with attention-deficit disorder. *Attention, 7*(3), 25–27.

Stormont-Spurgin, M. (1997). I lost my homework: Strategies for improving organization in students with ADHD. *Intervention in School & Clinic, 32*(5) 270–274.

The Importance of Peer Relationships

DuPaul, G. J., Bankert, C. L., & Ervin, R. A. (1994). Classwide peer tutoring: A school-based academic intervention for ADHD. *The ADHD Report, 2*(4), 4–5.

Frankel, F., & Feinberg, D. (2002). Social problems associated with ADHD vs. ODD in children referred for friendship problems. *Child Psychiatry & Human Development, 33*(2), 125–146.

Gardill, C. M., & DuPaul, G. J. (1996). Classroom strategies for managing students with attention-deficit/hyperactivity disorder. *Intervention in School & Clinic, 39*(3) 89–94.

Northup, J., & Broussard, C. (1995). The differential effects of teacher and peer attention on the disruptive classroom behavior of three children with a diagnosis of attention deficit hyperactivity. *Journal of Applied Behavior Analysis, 28*(2), 227–228.

Using Positive Reinforcement

Glass, C. S. (2001). Factors influencing teaching strategies used with children who display attention deficit hyperactivity disorder characteristics. *Education, 122*(1), 70–79.

Lock, J. (1996). Developmental considerations in the treatment of school-age boys with ADHD: An example of a group treatment approach. *Journal of the American Academy of Child & Adolescent Psychiatry, 35*(11), 1557–1559.

Meade, K., & Chandler, W. (2000). Mark's story part 2. *Attention, 7*(3), 29–33.

Reis, E. M. (2002). Attention deficit hyperactiviy disorder: Implications for the classroom teacher. *Journal of Instructional Psychology, 29*(3), 175–179.

Rosenberg, M. S., & Jackman, L. A. (2003). Development, implementation, and sustainability of comprehensive school-wide behavior management systems. *Intervention in School & Clinic, 39*(1), 10–21.

Teaching Students to Self-Monitor

Edwards, L. (1995). Effectiveness of self-management on attentional behavior and reading comprehension for children with attention deficit disorder. *Child & Family Behavior Therapy, 17*(2), 1–17.

Fraser, C., Belzner, R., & Conte, R. (1992). Attention deficit hyperactivity disorder and self-control: A single case study of the use of a timing device in the development of self-monitoring. *School Psychology International, 13*(4), 339–345.

Hoff, K. E., & DuPaul, G. J. (1998). Reducing disruptive behavior in general education classrooms: The use of self-management strategies. *School Psychology Review, 27*(2), 290–303.

Malian, I., & Nevin, A. (2002). A review of self-determination literature: Implications for practitioners. *Remedial and Special Education, 23*(2), 68–74.

Mathes, M. Y., & Bender, W. N. (1997). The effects of self-monitoring on children with attention-deficit/hyperactivity disorder who are receiving pharmacological interventions. *Remedial & Special Education, 18*(2), 121–128.

Paolitto, A. W. (2000). Differential utilization of problem solving strategies by children with ADHD. *The ADHD Report, 8*(3), 8–11.

Developing and Implementing Token Economy Systems

Barkley, R. A. (1996). 18 ways to make token systems more effective for ADHD children and teens. *The ADHD Report, 4*(4), 1–5.

Garrick Duhaney, L. M. (2003). A practical approach for managing the behaviors of students with ADD. *Intervention in School and Clinic, 38*(5), 267–279.

Luiselli, J. K. (1994). A multicomponent classroom intervention for independent academic productivity. *The ADHD Report, 2*(5), 5–7.

Reid, R. (1999). Attention deficit hyperactivity disorder: Effective methods for the classroom. *Focus on Exceptional Children, 32*(4), 1–19.

Using Graphic Organizers and Contracts

Ae-Hwa K., Beth A., Vaughn, S., Wanzek, J., & Shangjin Wei, J. (2004). Graphic organizers and their effects on the reading comprehension of students with LD: A synthesis of research. *Journal of Learning Disabilities, 37*(2), 105–118.

Baxendell, B. W. (2003). Consistent, coherent, creative: The 3 Cs of graphic organizers. *Teaching Exceptional Children, 35*(3), 46–53.

Hammill, D. D., & Bartel, N. R. (2004). *Teaching students with learning and behavior problems* (7th ed.). Austin, TX: PRO-ED.

Rief, S. (2000). AD/HD: Common academic difficulties & strategies that help. *Attention, 7*(2), 47–51.

Roberts, M., White, R., & McLaughlin, T. F. (1997). Useful classroom accommodations for teaching children with ADD and ADHD. *B.C. Journal of Special Education, 21,* 71–84.

Salend, S. J., Elhowers, H., & van Garderen, D. (2003). Educational interventions for students with ADD. *Intervention in School and Clinic, 38*(5), 280–288.

Teaching Study Skills

Conderman, G., & Koroghlanian, C. (2002). Writing test questions like a pro. *Intervention in School and Clinic, 38*(2), 83–87.

Faber, J. E., Morris, J. D., & Lieberman, M. G. (2000). The effect of note taking on ninth grade students' comprehension. *Reading Psychology, 21*(3), 257–270.

Schwartz, A. E. (2004). Scoring higher on math tests. *Education Digest, 69*(8), 39–44.

Wilson, N. S. (1986). Counselor interventions with low-achieving and underachieving elementary, middle, and high school students: A review of the literature. *Journal of Counseling & Development, 64*(10), 628–634.

Practical Ideas
That Really Work
for Students with ADHD

Second Edition

Grade 5 Through Grade 12

Kathleen McConnell • Gail R. Ryser

Evaluation Form

Name *Kelly Sanford*

Birth Date *11-14-92*   Age *12*

School *Moss Middle School*   Grade *7*

Rater *teacher—Ms. Watson*

Subject Area *Social Studies*

Dates Student Observed: From *8-20-04* To *10-1-04*

Amount of Time Spent with Student:

Per Day *50 min..* Per Week _____

DSM–IV–TR Diagnostic Criteria for Attention-Deficit/Hyperactivity Disorder

A. Either (1) or (2):

(1) six (or more) of the following symptoms of inattention have persisted for at least 6 months to a degree that is maladaptive and inconsistent with developmental level:

Inattention

(a) often fails to give close attention to details or makes careless mistakes in schoolwork, work, or other activities

(b) often has difficulty sustaining attention in tasks or play activities

(c) often does not seem to listen when spoken to directly

(d) often does not follow through on instructions and fails to finish schoolwork, chores, or duties in the workplace (not due to oppositional behavior or failure to understand instructions)

(e) often has difficulty organizing tasks and activities

(f) often avoids, dislikes, or is reluctant to engage in tasks that require sustained mental effort (such as schoolwork or homework)

(g) often loses things necessary for tasks or activities (e.g., toys, school assignments, pencils, books, tools)

(h) is often easily distracted by extraneous stimuli

(i) is often forgetful in daily activities

(2) six (or more) of the following symptoms of hyperactivity-impulsivity have persisted for at least 6 months to a degree that is maladaptive and inconsistent with developmental level:

Hyperactivity

(a) often fidgets with hands or feet or squirms in seat

(b) often leaves seat in classroom or in other situations in which remaining seated is expected

(c) often runs about or climbs excessively in situations in which it is inappropriate (in adolescents or adults, may be limited to subjective feelings of restlessness)

(d) often has difficulty playing or engaging in leisure activities quietly

(e) is often "on the go" or often acts as if "driven by a motor"

(f) often talks excessively

Impulsivity

(g) often blurts out answers before questions have been completed

(h) often has difficulty awaiting turn

(i) often interrupts or intrudes on others (e.g., butts into conversations or games)

Note. From the *Diagnostic and Statistical Manual of Mental Disorders–Fourth Edition–Text Revision*, 2000, Washington, DC: American Psychiatric Association. Copyright 2000 by American Psychiatric Association. Reprinted with permission.

Figure 1. Sample Evaluation Form, filled out for Kelly.

Rating Scale

DIRECTIONS

❶ Use the following scale to circle the appropriate number:

0 = *Never exhibits the behavior*

1 = *Rarely exhibits the behavior so it almost never interferes with the student's ability to function in the learning environment*

2 = *Sometimes exhibits the behavior so at times it interferes with the student's ability to function in the learning environment*

3 = *Consistently exhibits the behavior to the point it almost always interferes with the student's ability to function in the learning environment*

❷ Total the ratings and record in the Total box.

❸ Put a check in the Immediate Intervention column by the top three problems. (Give special consideration to those items with totals ≥ 6.)

❹ For each area checked, select up to three ideas from the Ideas Matrix on page 4. Write the idea number and start date for each idea in the blanks provided in the last column.

BEHAVIOR	RATING	TOTAL	IMMEDIATE INTERVENTION	IDEA NUMBER; START DATE

Rating columns: Never, Rarely, Sometimes, Consistently

Inattention

Makes careless mistakes
1 Turns in sloppy work. — 0 ①(1) 2 3
2 Gets low grades as a result of carelessness. — 0 ①(1) 2 3
3 Fails to give close attention to schoolwork. — 0 1 ②(2) 3
TOTAL: **4** | ○

Doesn't stay focused
1 Frequently shifts the focus of the conversation. — 0 ①(1) 2 3
2 Has difficulty sticking with a task through completion. — 0 1 ②(2) 3
3 Changes to a new activity before completing the previous activity. — 0 1 ②(2) 3
TOTAL: **5** | ○

Doesn't listen
1 Asks the teacher to repeat instructions. — 0 ①(1) 2 3
2 Has difficulty following multiple step directions. — 0 ①(1) 2 3
3 Seems to be daydreaming when spoken to directly. — 0 1 ②(2) 3
TOTAL: **4** | ○

Incomplete assignments
1 Daydreams instead of working on in-class assignments, even though he or she understands instructions. — 0 1 2 ③(3)
2 Completes only portions of assignments. — 0 1 2 ③(3)
3 Has difficulty following through on teacher requests. — 0 1 2 ③(3)
TOTAL: **9** | ✓ | 24 10-4-04

Unorganized
1 Has difficulty keeping track of assignments. — 0 1 ②(2) 3
2 Is a poor planner. — 0 1 2 ③(3)
3 Has an unorganized and messy notebook. — 0 1 ②(2) 3
TOTAL: **7** | ✓ | 5 10-21-04 / 23 10-21-04

Lacks sustained attention
1 Is off-task. — 0 1 ②(2) 3
2 Has difficulty concentrating. — 0 ①(1) 2 3
3 Has difficulty completing long-term projects. — 0 1 ②(2) 3
TOTAL: **5** | ○

Loses supplies
1 Loses homework assignments. — 0 1 ②(2) 3
2 Loses school supplies. — 0 1 ②(2) 3
3 Damages tools (e.g., calculator) necessary for completing schoolwork as a result of carelessness. — 0 ①(1) 2 3
TOTAL: **5** | ○

Easily distracted
1 Attends to what is happening outside the classroom instead of staying on task. — 0 ①(1) 2 3
2 Has trouble concentrating. — 0 1 ②(2) 3
3 Is easily distracted. — 0 1 ②(2) 3
TOTAL: **5** | ○

Forgetful
1 Forgets to take important papers home or give them to parents. — 0 1 ②(2) 3
2 Forgets to study for a test or quiz. — 0 ①(1) 2 3
3 Misplaces pencils, pens, and papers while in class. — 0 1 ②(2) 3
TOTAL: **5** | ○

2

Figure 1. Continued.

BEHAVIOR	RATING	TOTAL	IMMEDIATE INTERVENTION	IDEA NUMBER; START DATE

Hyperactivity

	Never	Rarely	Sometimes	Consistently

Fidgets, wiggles
1 Has difficulty sitting still in desk. 0 (1) 2 3
2 Drums fingers or taps pencil or other objects. 0 1 (2) 3
3 Wiggles or squirms excessively. 0 (1) 2 3

TOTAL: **4** IMMEDIATE INTERVENTION: ◯

Out of seat
1 Leaves seat without permission. 0 (1) 2 3
2 Gets up to wander around the room. 0 (1) 2 3
3 Has difficulty staying seated during presentations or special events. (0) 1 2 3

TOTAL: **2** IMMEDIATE INTERVENTION: ◯

Excessive movement
1 Is restless. 0 (1) 2 3
2 Jumps or climbs on furniture. (0) 1 2 3
3 Runs in the hallways when passing from class to class. (0) 1 2 3

TOTAL: **1** IMMEDIATE INTERVENTION: ◯

Difficulty with quiet activities
1 Shifts from one activity to another during free time. 0 (1) 2 3
2 Has difficulty playing quietly. (0) 1 2 3
3 Is easily excited. 0 (1) 2 3

TOTAL: **2** IMMEDIATE INTERVENTION: ◯

Never stops moving
1 Is "on-the-go." 0 (1) 2 3
2 Engages in physically dangerous activities. (0) 1 2 3
3 Has trouble slowing down or relaxing. 0 (1) 2 3

TOTAL: **2** IMMEDIATE INTERVENTION: ◯

Talks excessively
1 Makes excessive noise during quiet activities. 0 (1) 2 3
2 Talks too much. 0 1 (2) 3
3 Dominates conversations so that others cannot "get a word in edgewise." 0 (1) 2 3

TOTAL: **4** IMMEDIATE INTERVENTION: ◯

Impulsivity

Speaks without permission
1 Blurts out answers. 0 1 (2) 3
2 Has difficulty waiting for directions before proceeding. 0 1 (2) 3
3 Has trouble waiting for teachers or others to complete their question before responding. 0 1 (2) 3

TOTAL: **6** IMMEDIATE INTERVENTION: ✓ IDEA NUMBER; START DATE: 6 11-1-04

Can't wait for turn
1 Has difficulty taking turns when playing games. 0 (1) 2 3
2 Makes comments out of turn. 0 1 (2) 3
3 Fails to wait for his or her turn. 0 (1) 2 3

TOTAL: **4** IMMEDIATE INTERVENTION: ◯

Interrupts others; grabs materials
1 Interrupts others in casual conversation. 0 (1) 2 3
2 Intrudes on others in social situations. 0 (1) 2 3
3 Grabs objects from others. (0) 1 2 3

TOTAL: **2** IMMEDIATE INTERVENTION: ◯

3

Figure 1. Continued.

Ideas Matrix

Ideas	Inattention									Hyperactivity						Impulsivity		
	Makes Careless Mistakes	Doesn't Stay Focused	Doesn't Listen	Incomplete Assignments	Unorganized	Lacks Sustained Attention	Loses Supplies	Easily Distracted	Forgetful	Fidgets, Wiggles	Out of Seat	Excessive Movement	Quiet Activities	Never Stops Moving	Talks Excessively	Speaks Without Permission	Can't Wait for Turn	Interrupts and Grabs
1 Positive Reinforcement	●	●	●	●	●	●	●	●	●	●	●	●	●	●	●	●	●	●
2 Behavior Monitoring Forms	●	●	●	●	●	●	●	●	●	●	●	●	●	●	●	●	●	●
3 Bragging Buddies		●		●		●		●										
4 Countdown to Good Behavior	●	●	●	●	●	●	●	●	●	●	●	●	●	●	●	●	●	●
5 Good Habits To Get Organized				●	●		●		●									
6 Triple T		●	●			●		●		●					●	●	●	●
7 Visual Warnings									●	●	●					●	●	●
8 Consistently Consistent	●	●	●	●	●	●	●	●	●	●	●	●	●	●	●	●	●	●
9 Buddy Out										●	●	●	●	●	●	●	●	●
10 Nonverbal Signal System		●	●	●		●		●										
11 Name Dropping		●	●			●		●										
12 Nonverbal Cues		●	●	●		●		●										
13 Contestant Cards		●	●			●		●										
14 Self-Checklist	●	●	●	●	●	●	●	●	●	●	●	●		●	●			
15 Random Checks		●	●			●		●		●	●	●		●	●			
16 Three Bs										●	●	●		●			●	●
17 Quiet Corner		●				●		●		●	●	●	●	●	●	●	●	●
18 Earplugs or Headphones		●				●		●		●	●	●		●				
19 Modify Movements										●	●	●	●	●				
20 Let Students Leave		●						●		●								
21 Give Me Five										●		●		●		●	●	●
22 Self-Management		●		●		●		●		●	●	●	●	●	●	●	●	●
23 Write a Contract	●			●	●		●		●									
24 Homework Forms		●		●	●	●			●									
25 Team Checkers			●	●	●		●		●									
26 Test-Taking Strategies	●	●				●		●										
27 Date Reminders		●	●	●	●				●									
28 Rewards for Neatness	●	●			●													
29 Mnemonics	●		●	●	●				●									
30 Boundaries	●	●		●	●	●		●										
31 Basic Graphic Organizers	●	●		●	●													
32 Cause/Effect and Sequencing	●	●		●	●													
33 Problem-Solver	●	●		●	●													
34 Compare-and-Contrast	●	●		●	●													
35 Post-it Notes	●	●		●	●													
36 Not Just Underlining	●	●		●	●				●									
37 Note Taking Made Easy	●	●		●	●				●									

4

Figure 1. Continued.

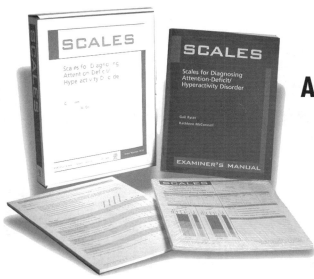

SCALES
Scales for Diagnosing Attention-Deficit/Hyperactivity Disorder

The authors of *Practical Ideas That Really Work for Students with ADHD* are proud to announce the creation of a norm-referenced measure for identifying students ages 5 through 18 with ADHD.

If you find the rating scale that accompanies Practical Ideas useful, you will want to purchase this norm-referenced rating scale.

Notable Features

➤ the flexibility to evaluate a child's behavior using either normative benchmarks or DSM–IV–TR criteria

➤ the inclusion of four separate normative samples

➤ the inclusion of items that immediately address the child's ability to function within both school and home environments (i.e., it has two separate forms, one for the home environment and the other for the school setting)

The SCALES is modeled after the guidelines for ADHD in the *Diagnostic and Statistical Manual of Mental Disorders–Fourth Edition–Text Revision* (DSM–IV–TR). Maintaining the internal coherency of those criteria, it evaluates the child's behavior using three subtests to measure inattention, hyperactivity, and impulsivity. In addition, the American Academy of Pediatrics' *2000 Practice Guidelines for the Diagnosis and Evaluation of ADHD* was heavily consulted.

Reliability and Validity

Reliability and validity for the SCALES are strong. The average internal consistency coefficient ranged from .88 to .96. Criterion-prediction validity studies were conducted using the *Conners' Rating Scales* and the *Attention-Deficit/ Hyperactivity Disorder Test*.

Review

The SCALES was reviewed in Buros's *Fifteenth Mental Measurements Yearbook* (Law, 2003). The reviewer had this comment to make, "The SCALES is a well-developed, reliable, and potentially valid instrument for use in assessing attention-deficit/hyperactivity disorder." (p. 769)

The SCALES Complete Kit includes: Examiner's Manual, 25 Summary/School Rating Scale Forms, and 25 Home Rating Scale Forms, all in a sturdy storage box. (2002)

SCALES
Scales for Diagnosing
Attention-Deficit/Hyperactivity Disorder

Gail R. Ryser ❖ Kathleen McConnell

10% Discount on the SCALES

ORDER FORM

Please send me:

QTY.		PRICE	TOTAL
_____	SCALES Complete Kit (#9670)	$86.00	_____
_____	SCALES Examiner's Manual (#9671)	$51.00	_____
_____	SCALES Summary/School Rating Scale Forms (#9672)	$25.00	_____
_____	SCALES Home Rating Scale Forms (#9673)	$15.00	_____

SUBTOTAL	_____
MINUS 10% DISCOUNT	_____
Shipping and Handling Charges:	_____
(United States 10%; Canada 15%; Foreign 20%)	
Texas residents add 8.25% sales tax.	_____
(U.S. Funds Only) **TOTAL**	_____

All products sold on 30-day approval. ❖ Prices subject to change without notice.

Return form to:

PRO-ED, Inc.
8700 Shoal Creek Blvd.
Austin, Texas 78757
800/897-3202 ❖ Fax 800/397-7633
www.proedinc.com

_____ _____
DATE   DAYTIME TELEPHONE

BILL TO _____
CREDIT CARD OR PURCHASE ORDER BILLING ADDRESS

_____

_____

_____

PAYMENT METHOD
☐ Purchase Order ☐ Check ☐ American Express
☐ Discover ☐ MasterCard ☐ VISA

_____ _____
CREDIT CARD NUMBER   EXP. DATE

_____
SIGNATURE

SHIP TO _____
FILL IN ONLY IF DIFFERENT FROM BILLING ADDRESS

_____

_____

_____

Idea 1
Positive Reinforcement

The term *positive reinforcement* means a consequence that increases a behavior. Teachers who use positive reinforcement effectively often see great improvement in students' behavior. Below are some simple ways of making your reinforcement work better.

Here are a few guidelines.

❶ Be specific about the behavior you want. Pick one behavior at a time and specify an action verb. For example:
- Raise your hand before talking.
- Ask for help when you don't understand.
- Stay quiet for at least 5 minutes.

❷ Use praise statements that describe the specific behavior you want. For example:
- Thanks for waiting so quietly.
- Great job getting started so quickly.

It's still okay to make more general statements like "Super" or "Good work," but more specific verbal statements help students with ADHD to keep focused on the most important behavior.

❸ Create a menu of reinforcers and change it often. We have provided an example of a menu or you can create your own.
- If you copy the menu on heavy paper and laminate it, you can change the menu daily or weekly by checking off different boxes.

❹ Instead of using the menu, let students roll a reinforcement die.
- Write the reinforcers on the cube template we have provided and make a die.

❺ Keep coupons in a jar and let students draw their reinforcements. Use the coupons we have provided or make your own.

❻ Make sure you (and anyone else working with the student) reinforce consistently. It is very important that you keep using positive reinforcement even after the student's behavior begins to improve.

Reinforcement Menu for Today

- ❏ Run errands today
- ❏ Water the plants
- ❏ Do half of an assignment
- ❏ Add 2 bonus points to a quiz
- ❏ Have talk time with friends
- ❏ Get treat at the end of the day
- ❏ Get reading time for the whole class
- ❏ Take extra break time for the whole class
- ❏ Grab something from the grab bag
- ❏ Use the computer for extra time

_____

_____

_____

_____

Idea 1

Cube Template

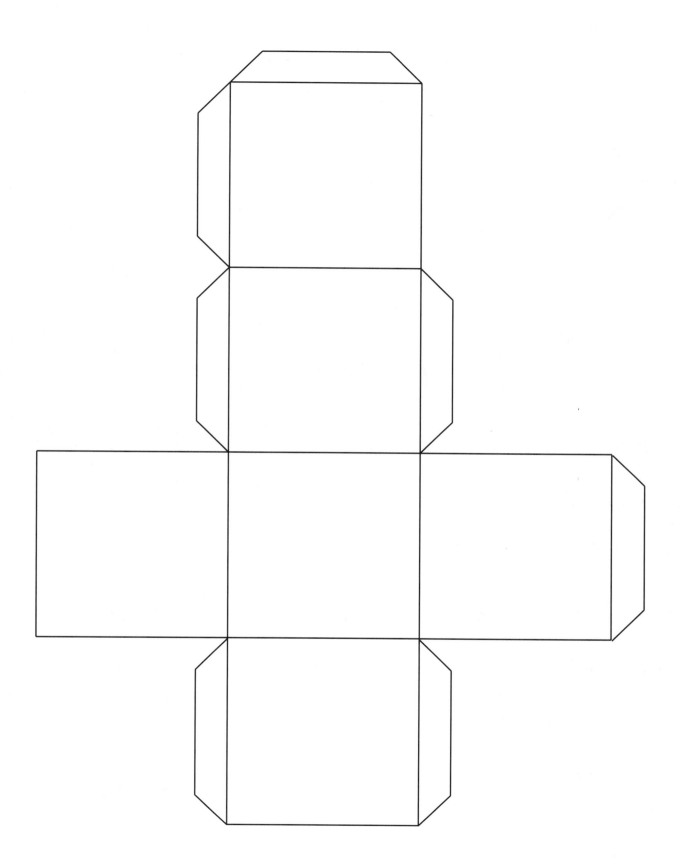

13

Office assistant	One question answered on next test	Do half of an assignment
5 bonus points added to next quiz	10 minutes extra computer time	Movie on Friday
10 minutes talk time	Break time for the whole class	Popcorn on Friday

Idea 1

Idea 2
Behavior Monitoring Forms

Students with ADHD often benefit from feedback about their behavior, especially positive reinforcement when that behavior is appropriate and desirable. Behavior monitoring forms (also called daily report cards) help students maintain their good patterns of behavior. The forms also help teachers respond to those behaviors with consistent positive reinforcement. Each time students do well, the teacher has an opportunity to praise and reward. We have provided a form that is quick and easy to complete and can follow students from class to class.

Here's how to use the Daily Tracking Form.

This form tracks three specific behaviors and rates a student's overall behavior throughout a school day or in a selected class. The teacher checks the appropriate box to indicate that the student was on time to class, prepared for class, and whether homework was assigned. Additionally, the teacher rates the student's behavior as excellent, fair, or poor by using the key at the bottom of the chart and signing or initialing the last box. This form should go home daily with the student so that the parent can provide a reinforcer for appropriate behavior.

Name _Jim Russell_

Daily Tracking Form

Date _April 7_

Class	On Time?		Prepared?		Homework Assigned?		Behavior			Teacher's Initials
	Yes	No	Yes	No	Yes	No	Excellent	Fair	Poor	
Social Studies	☑	☐	☑	☐	☑	☐				
Math	☐	☑	☑	☐	☑	☐	☐	☑	☐	LA
P. E.	☑	☐	☐	☑	☐	☑	☐	☐	☑	PO
Science	☐	☑	☐	☑	☑	☐	☐	☑	☐	DH
	☐	☐	☐	☑	☑	☐	☑	☐	☐	VW
	☐	☐	☐	☐	☐	☐	☐	☐	☐	

Key for Behavior:

Excellent
1. Consistently follows classroom rules.
2. Actively listens.
3. Volunteers in class discussions/activities.
4. Speaks respectfully to others.

Fair
1. Follows classroom rules most of the time.
2. Listens at least 75% of the time.
3. Participates when called upon.
4. Speaks respectfully to others some of the time.

Poor
1. Does not follow classroom rules.
2. Does not listen to the teacher.
3. Does not participate in classroom discussions/activities.
4. Is not respectful to others.

Note. The Daily Tracking Form was adapted from *The Tough Kid Tool Box* (pp. 93 and 111), by W. R. Jenson, G. Rhode, and H. K. Reavis, 1994–1995, Longmont, CO: Sopris West. Copyright 1994–1995 by William R. Jenson, Ginger Rhode, and H. Kenton Reavis. Adapted with permission.

Daily Tracking Form

Name _____   Date _____

Class	On Time?		Prepared?		Homework Assigned?		Behavior			Teacher's Initials
	Yes	No	Yes	No	Yes	No	Excellent	Fair	Poor	
	☐	☐	☐	☐	☐	☐	☐	☐	☐	
	☐	☐	☐	☐	☐	☐	☐	☐	☐	
	☐	☐	☐	☐	☐	☐	☐	☐	☐	
	☐	☐	☐	☐	☐	☐	☐	☐	☐	
	☐	☐	☐	☐	☐	☐	☐	☐	☐	

Key for Behavior:

Excellent
1. Consistently follows classroom rules.
2. Actively listens.
3. Volunteers in class discussions/activities.
4. Speaks respectfully to others.

Fair
1. Follows classroom rules most of the time.
2. Listens at least 75% of the time.
3. Participates when called upon.
4. Speaks respectfully to others some of the time.

Poor
1. Does not follow classroom rules.
2. Does not listen to the teacher.
3. Does not participate in classroom discussions/activities.
4. Is not respectful to others.

Idea 2

Idea 3
Bragging Buddies

To build group cohesiveness and help students see themselves as part of the solution instead of part of the problem in the classroom, teach your students to become Bragging Buddies.

Here's what to do.

❶ First, write or print brag phrases on cards. Focus on simple, fun phrases students can use to encourage each other. Set the cards in the middle of the students' tables or desks and post them on the wall so that they are always visible. Start with two basic brags: "Good job" and "Good try."

❷ When a student makes a correct statement or gets something right, students say "Good job." If the answer is incorrect, someone still offers a brag: "Good try." After students get the hang of it, gradually add other brags so that they have lots of choices but are not overwhelmed.

❸ Make sure that all students praise each other. You can do this by passing out Bragging Buddy tickets at the beginning of the day or class, one per student. After a student praises a peer, he or she puts a ticket in the jar and is qualified for the Bragging Bonus. The Bragging Bonus is randomly selected by drawing a ticket, which entitles the student to a candy bar, ice cream bar at lunchtime, lunch with friends, pizza party at the end of 2 weeks, or other treat.

❹ After every student comment, regardless of whether it is correct, students should reinforce each other with a brag. Here are some ideas:

- Nice try!
- I like it!
- Way to go!
- That's super!
- You can do it!
- You got it!

❺ After your students have become good Bragging Buddies, set aside a few minutes each Monday morning to have them decide on the brags for the week.

18

Idea 3

This week's brag

Idea 4

Countdown to Good Behavior

Here's a group management strategy that works for all students, regardless of age. It includes a systematic way of warning students that encourages consistency and doesn't provide teacher attention for misbehavior.

Here's how it works.

❶ Create a sign that is large enough for all students in the class to see. The sign should have the numbers 5-4-3-2-1 in vertical order. If possible, use bright, appealing colors and make sure the sign is large enough for all students to see from anywhere in the classroom. We have provided a form that you can enlarge for class use or use as is for individual students.

❷ Attach a large clip or arrow on the side of the sign by the number 5. This will be your starting point while teaching.

➡ 5
4
3
2
1

 **Tip:**

Use 5-4-3-2-1 the first semester and 3-2-1 after students have had time to learn the system and practice following the rules.

❸ Decide on your target behaviors. Start with the basics necessary for direct instruction:
  • Stay seated
  • Raise your hand before talking

Note. Countdown to Good Behavior is from *Practical Ideas That Really Work for Students with Disruptive, Defiant, or Difficult Behaviors, Preschool through Grade 4,* by K. McConnell, G. Ryser, and J. R. Patton, 2002, Austin, TX: PRO-ED, Inc. Copyright 2002 by PRO-ED, Inc. Reprinted with permission. Countdown to Good Behavior was originally adapted from *Project Ride: Responding to Individual Differences in Education, Elementary School Edition,* by R. Beck, 1996, Longmont, CO: Sopris West. Copyright 1996 by Sopris West. Adapted with permission.

❹ Explain to your students that if they have to be warned four or fewer times during the lesson, the whole class will have a special activity. (Four or fewer warnings is indicated by the clip being on any number; remove the clip on the fifth warning.) You can create a menu of activities that your students really like, including:
- Extra break time
- Five minutes to talk to friends at the end of class
- Reading time
- Extra drinks at the water fountain
- Popcorn party on Friday

❺ Begin your direct instruction lesson. Keep it short the first few times (5 to 10 minutes). If students fail to follow either of the two rules, move the clip down from the 5 to the 4. Look directly at the student who has talked out or been out of his or her seat but do not stop teaching to reprimand him or her or otherwise provide attention.

❻ Finally, at the end of the lesson, compliment students if they still have a low-enough number and provide the selected reinforcer. If there have been too many warnings, try again.

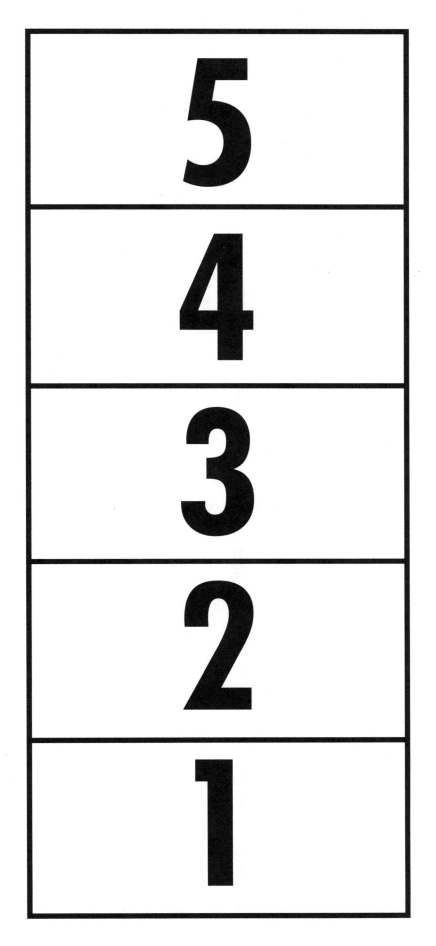

Idea 4

Idea 5
Good Habits To Get Organized

Organization is a critical skill for all students, but for students with ADHD, organization can be virtually nonexistent. It is not unusual for students with ADHD to have important papers stuck haphazardly into notebooks, folded up in pockets, or wadded up in the corners of their rooms or backpacks. It is distressing for students to get poor grades because they never get their completed homework turned in on time, and it is equally distressing for teachers to give students low grades because students can't seem to turn their work in on time, if at all. The sooner organization becomes a habit for students with ADHD, the sooner they can be successful in school and in life. This idea contains a method to teach organizational habits, followed by several good habits to help students get organized.

Here are the steps for teaching organizational habits.

❶ Develop a mnemonic to teach the organizational habit. In this example, teach students to bring their materials (paper, pens, or pencils) to class. We call it Big Purple People Eater (**B**ring **P**aper and **P**ens **E**very day).

❷ Introduce BPPE by showing the Big Purple People Eater picture we have provided. Discuss with students the importance of bringing supplies to class everyday. Next brainstorm with the class what happens when students forget to bring their supplies.

❸ Do several days of choral responding in which the entire class repeats Big Purple People Eater while placing their paper and pens on their desks. Later, use choral responding periodically.

❹ To reinforce, use the BPPE coupons we have included to reward students who bring their supplies to class everyday. Allow students to turn in their coupons for rewards.

❺ Repeat this process with other organizational habits you want to teach.

Tip:

Copy the Big Purple People Eater on purple paper and the Chomp Red Strawberries on red paper.

Note. This idea is based on a teaching method from "Looking for Betty Crocker Not Martha Stewart: Practical Suggestions for Busy Teachers of Kids with Challenging Behaviors," K. Callicott, 2003, *Beyond Behavior, 13*(1), pp. 32–34.

Here are some good habits to get organized.

❶ Have one notebook and folder for each subject. Color-code each subject and make sure that everything related to that subject is the same color. For example, if science is green, then the notebook, folder, and highlighter are also green.

❷ Use the folder for assignments. On one side of the folder write in big letters TO DO. On the other side write TO TURN IN. Teach students to check the folder two times a day: at home (TO DO) and at the beginning of class (TO TURN IN).

❸ Have students write their names, e-mail addresses, schools, subjects, teachers' names, and other pertinent information in every notebook and folder. This increases the chance of the notebook and folder being returned to the student they get lost.

❹ Use every Friday as de-clutter day. Make students go through their notebooks and folders and throw away papers that are not needed, punch holes in and file papers that are important, and place partially completed homework assignments in their folder on the TO DO side.

❺ Provide students with a syllabus for each marking period with the dates for exams and major assignments marked in large bold print. Laminate and punch three holes in them, and at the beginning of each marking period, have students put them in the front of their notebooks.

❻ Write assignments on the board at the beginning or midway through the class. Don't wait until the last minute to tell students the assignment, because it increases the probability that it won't get recorded.

❼ Have students form homework buddies at the beginning of the year. Students can call their homework buddies if they forget their homework assignments. Change homework buddies frequently so that one student doesn't get stuck with the habitual forgetter.

❽ Stress the importance of transition. Transitions are often when things get lost, homework doesn't get recorded, and books get left behind. Teach students Chomp Red Strawberries (**C**heck to make sure you have your supplies for the next class, **R**ecord the assignment or other important information, **S**tore your books and supplies in your backpack). A picture and coupons are provided.

Big Purple People Eater

Bring **P**aper and **P**ens **E**very day

Idea 5

Big Purple People Eater

Bring **P**aper and **P**ens **E**very day

Big Purple People Eater

Bring **P**aper and **P**ens **E**very day

Big Purple People Eater

Bring **P**aper and **P**ens **E**very day

Big Purple People Eater

Bring **P**aper and **P**ens **E**very day

Big Purple People Eater

Bring **P**aper and **P**ens **E**very day

Big Purple People Eater

Bring **P**aper and **P**ens **E**very day

Big Purple People Eater

Bring **P**aper and **P**ens **E**very day

Big Purple People Eater

Bring **P**aper and **P**ens **E**very day

Idea 5

Chomp Red Strawberries

Check to make sure you have your supplies for the next class.

Record the assignment or other important information.

Store your books and supplies in your backpack.

Idea 5

Chomp Red
Strawberries

Check, Record, Store

Chomp Red
Strawberries

Check, Record, Store

Chomp Red
Strawberries

Check, Record, Store

Chomp Red
Strawberries

Check, Record, Store

Chomp Red
Strawberries

Check, Record, Store

Chomp Red
Strawberries

Check, Record, Store

Chomp Red
Strawberries

Check, Record, Store

Chomp Red
Strawberries

Check, Record, Store

Idea 5

Idea 6
Triple T

Triple T—Teacher Talk Time—helps students stay quiet and focused during direct instruction. Before you begin, locate a timer, a large clear plastic tub or jar, and your Yes/No tickets (see forms for this section). The Yes tickets should be copied on bright green paper and the No tickets on bright red paper.

Here's what to do.

1 Explain to students that during direct instruction time (Triple T), it is important that the teacher does the talking. However, the time will be limited and will not exceed a specified limit.

2 Explain the two rules during Triple T:
- Only the teacher talks, unless students are called on by name to answer a question.
- Students must stay seated.

3 Set a timer for an appropriate amount of direct instruction time. For young students, try 5–10 minutes. For older students, try 10–20 minutes. If your students are distracted by the ticking timer, buy an inexpensive battery timer or set a watch that has a beeper. Tell your students that you absolutely promise to stop talking when the timer goes off, even if you are not completely finished. (You can always take a short break, then begin another Triple T session.)

Note. Part of this idea was adapted from *TGIF: But What Will I Do on Monday?* (p. 23), by S. L. Fister and K. A. Kemp, 1995, Longmont, CO: Sopris West. Copyright 1995 by Susan L. Fister and Karen A. Kemp. Adapted with permission.

❹ As you lecture, explain, or demonstrate, use the Yes/No tickets to give students visible feedback on how they are doing following the two rules. Every 2 to 3 minutes, put a Yes ticket in the jar if students are following the two rules and a No ticket in if someone breaks a rule. Do not interrupt your discussion to reprimand, warn, or remind. Just use the tickets.

❺ Finally, after the session, praise students for following the rules. At the end of the class period, day, or week (depending on the age of your students), make a big fuss about reaching into the jar with eyes closed and pulling out a ticket. A No means no reward, but a Yes means the entire class gets a goodie. Consider these options for class rewards:
- Extra recess or conversation time
- A night off from homework
- Extra points on the class participation average
- Snacks or soft drinks during seatwork time (Students can bring their own.)
- A quick game

Idea 6

Idea 6

Idea 7
Visual Warnings

For students in the intermediate grades, this two-part strategy works very well. The first part of the system is a structured visual warning system. If a student is disruptive during instruction, the teacher walks to the student's desk and places a bright yellow yield sign on it. If the disruption continues, the red stop sign is used next. Both are placed on the desk without discussion and without interrupting instruction. When the lesson is over, the student is required to write on his or her Behavior Sheet why the signs were given (i.e., what class rule was broken) and the consequence for breaking the rule. After a predetermined number of infractions are recorded, a system of consequences is implemented, including perhaps a student–teacher–parent conference or a loss of privileges. Because the strategy is used without discussion, it must be explained and modeled several times *before* it is used, giving students a chance to practice their responses. The class rules and corresponding consequenses for breaking the rules should be reviewed periodically, and they should be posted in the classroom.

We suggest you give each student a Behavior Sheet to keep in their notebooks at the beginning of the week. At the end of the week, collect all of the Behavior Sheets (whether or not they were used) to keep for documentation purposes.

 Tip:

Copy the yield sign on bright yellow paper and the stop sign on red. Laminate both so they can be used repeatedly.

Note. Idea provided by and used with permission of Kim Hill, fourth-grade teacher, Pine Tree Intermediate School, Longview, TX.

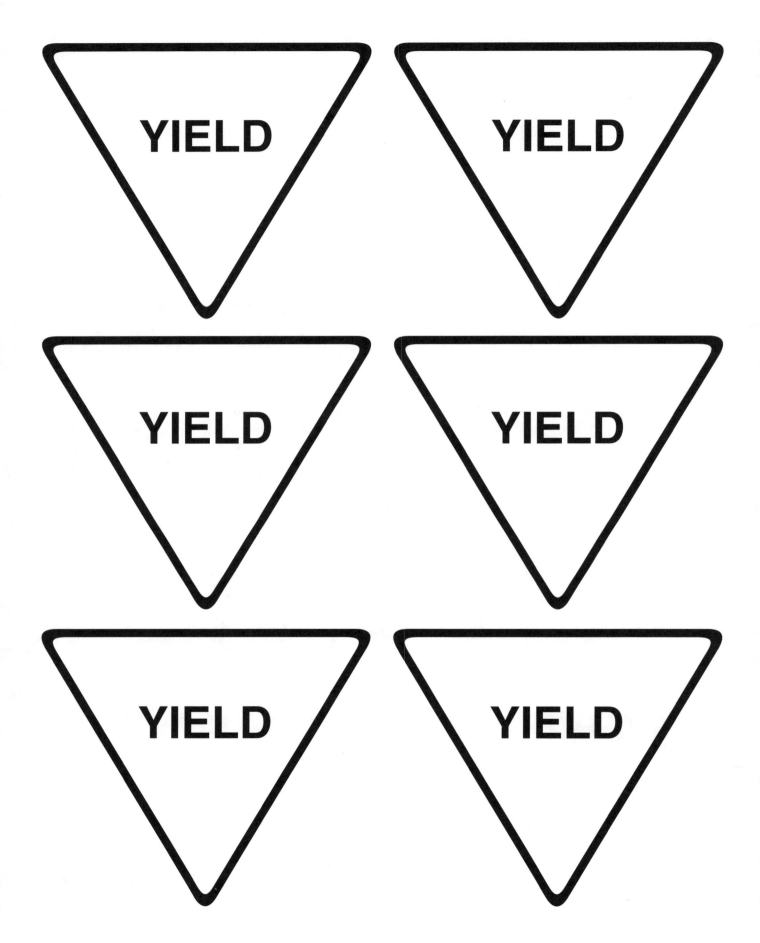

38

39

Name _____   Week of _____

Behavior Sheet

Day	Class Rule	Consequence
_____	_____	_____
_____	_____	_____
_____	_____	_____
_____	_____	_____
_____	_____	_____
_____	_____	_____
_____	_____	_____
_____	_____	_____
_____	_____	_____
_____	_____	_____
_____	_____	_____

Idea 7

Idea 8
Consistently Consistent

When using consequences with students who have ADHD, teachers should be consistently consistent. When teachers inconsistently apply consequences for misbehavior, students may continue to "get away with" misbehavior, or they may feel that they are being treated unfairly, which could result in ineffective consequences. A simple chart that can help teachers be consistently consistent with students is provided.

Here's how to use the Consistent Consequence Chart.

❶ First, copy the chart onto a transparency, so that it can be projected and easily seen by all students in the class.

❷ Across the top of the chart, write the continuum of consequences for misbehavior in the classroom. For example, the first intervention might be the "Look" (purposeful eye contact and a stern look that says, "Stop it"). The next consequence could be a verbal reminder. If the misbehavior continues, the next step might be a brief one-to-one conference in the hallway, followed by lunch detention, and then a call to parents.

The list of consequences should reflect what each teacher has decided to use and will actually implement. The teacher should write his or her consequences simply and briefly. We recommend 4 to 6 steps, since using more may allow too much disruption and make it difficult to maintain order in the classroom.

❸ Down the left side of the chart, write the name of each student, in alphabetical order. Secondary teachers who have more than one class should fill in one chart for each section they teach.

Consistent Consequence Chart

	Look	Verbal Reminder	1:1 Conference	Lunch Detention	Call Parents	
	1	2	3	4	5	6
	X	X	X			
Alice						
Barton	X					
Bachi	X	X				
Delbert						
Georgia						
Ingrid		X	X	X		
Joshua						
Jane		X	X			
Kathy						
Keishah						
Lamont						
Moses						
Pat						
Penny						

♦ When a student misbehaves, the teacher should implement his or her consequence. Immediately after the consequence, put an "X" in the appropriate box on the chart, so each student knows where he or she stands in the system. Just seeing the progression of consequences is enough to help many students with ADHD control themselves. The impact on teachers should also be positive, because they will talk less, remember what happened in their busy classrooms, and be consistently consistent when using consequences.

Consistent Consequence Chart

	1	2	3	4	5	6

Idea 8

Idea 9
Buddy Out

Sometimes, students with ADHD demonstrate behavior so disruptive that it interferes with the other students' learning or the teacher's instruction. When this happens, teachers need some realistic options for dealing with the behavior quickly and effectively. One such option is Buddy Out. This is a great strategy for secondary students, especially those who are impulsive and need time to calm down but who may not need to be sent to the office. Buddy Out gives the teacher and the other students some relief while the disruptive student gets a chance to regain his or her composure.

Here's how Buddy Out works.

❶ Teachers choose a partner teacher (a Buddy) whose classroom is close to theirs (next door or in the same hallway), and each Buddy Classroom should have a study carrel or desk in a quiet corner to use for students sent to Buddy Out.

❷ If a student has trouble with self-control and continues with disruptive behavior after warnings by the teacher, the teacher fills out a Buddy Out Card and asks the student to take it to the Buddy teacher's classroom.

❸ The Buddy Out Card states the specific amount of time the student should remain in the Buddy classroom and the reason for the student's Buddy Out. The student can either work on his or her assignment in the Buddy teacher's classroom or on independent work. (Teachers should prepare packets of independent work for Buddy teachers so that students have something to keep them busy and calm them down.)

> ### Buddy Out Card
> Date __May 14__
>
> __Dudley Mars__ is being sent from __Mr. Goodnight__ 's classroom to
> (STUDENT'S NAME) (SENDING BUDDY)
> __Ms. Reid__ 's classroom to Buddy Out.
> (RECEIVING BUDDY)
>
> This student should stay for   5   10   (15)   20   25   30   minutes.
> (CIRCLE ONE)
>
> The reason for the Buddy Out is:
> ☐ Too much talking
> ☑ Out of seat
> ☐ Bothering others
> ☐ Other: _____

❹ When the assigned time period is over, the Buddy teacher asks the student to return to his or her regular classroom.

If necessary, students buddying out can be assigned an escort. They can also complete the "How Did I Do?" self-evaluation form as a follow-up to the process.

Buddy Out Card

Date _____

_____ is being sent from _____'s classroom to
(STUDENT'S NAME)   (SENDING BUDDY)

_____'s classroom to Buddy Out.
(RECEIVING BUDDY)

This student should stay for   5   10   15   20   25   30   minutes.

(CIRCLE ONE)

The reason for the Buddy Out is:

❐ Too much talking

❐ Out of seat

❐ Bothering others

❐ Other: _____

Buddy Out Card

Date _____

_____ is being sent from _____'s classroom to
(STUDENT'S NAME)   (SENDING BUDDY)

_____'s classroom to Buddy Out.
(RECEIVING BUDDY)

This student should stay for   5   10   15   20   25   30   minutes.

(CIRCLE ONE)

The reason for the Buddy Out is:

❐ Too much talking

❐ Out of seat

❐ Bothering others

❐ Other: _____

Idea 9

Name _____   Date _____

How Did I Do?

How did I do on _____ ?

(Circle a number.)

1	2	3
Great	Okay	Not very well

What should I do differently next time?

_____

_____

Name _____   Date _____

How Did I Do?

How did I do on _____ ?

(Circle a number.)

1	2	3
Great	Okay	Not very well

What should I do differently next time?

_____

_____

Idea 9

Idea 10
Nonverbal Signal System

For quiet communication, students can use large signal cards that are attached to the front of their desks. The green side of the card can have a message that indicates that the student is working and does not need assistance. The flip side of the card, copied on red paper, can say "I need help." Either tape the cards to the front of students' desks so that they can flip them up when needed, or use Velcro to fasten the cards to the top corner of the desk.

To use signals that are less obvious, both the student and the teacher can use smaller cards to communicate back and forth. Laminate the cards, put them on a key ring or plastic bracelet, and teach students to hold up a card when they have a question or need help. Then, use the teacher's set to signal back to students, letting them know that you have seen them and will get to them as soon as possible.

I'm working hard.

 Tip:

For students who need larger or more visible signals, use two plastic-coated paper cups, one red and the other green. Glue or tape them together so that the bottoms of the cups are touching. Students can set them with the green side up when all is going well and the red side up when they need assistance.

I'm working hard.

Can you help me?

Can you
help me?

I'm working
hard.

?

ASAP

SOS

In a Minute

I Need Help

Need Help?

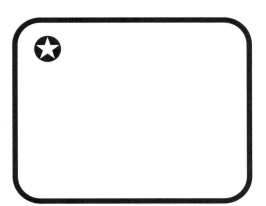

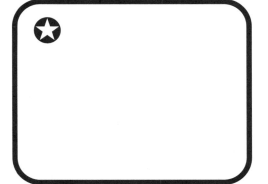

Idea 10

Idea 11
Name Dropping

When students with ADHD have trouble attending, teachers can try Name Dropping. Name Dropping is the conscious, purposeful use of students' names to increase attention.

Here are some of the strategies.

❶ Use the student's name two or three times in a row.

When students are off task and you are having trouble getting them to pay attention, use their name and ask them two or three questions in succession. ("Nicole, what do we mean by conflict?" "Nicole, what is the conflict in this story?" "Nicole, tell us why the conflict is happening.") After two or three questions, students often tire of your attention, sit up, and start to listen.

❷ Begin questions with a name.

While teachers should not always begin questions with a name, it is a good way to secure the attention of students with ADHD. Pause, say the student's name, and then ask the question slowly.

❸ Use the student's name when providing praise, but not when correcting.

This is an idea that sometimes works with those students who will do anything for attention. When this is the case, make sure that you make eye contact, smile, and use the student's name when he or she has done something correctly or behaved especially well. However, if you have to correct the student, move in close, give a verbal reminder or warning without using his or her name, and then quickly move away. This takes practice, but it can work well.

Idea 12
Nonverbal Cues

Students can benefit from nonverbal reminders, which also have the advantage of not interrupting instruction.

Here are three methods to use.

❶ Meet privately with the student and agree on an individualized gesture that will be used only for him or her. The gesture could be a tap on the shoulder, a finger to the lips (like a "shhhh" sign, or a raised hand or finger). When the student sees the teacher use the gesture, he or she should get back to work without talking.

❷ Signal the student with the small cue cards. As the teacher moves around the room, he or she can cue a student who is off task by simply placing a card on the student's desk. We suggest copying the card on brightly colored stock paper and laminating it before use, so that it is visible and reusable.

Back
to
Work

Get
Busy

Pay
Attention

Get
Started

Eyes On
the
Teacher

1 • 2 • 3
Go

Open
Your
Book

Time
to
Begin

58

Idea 13
Contestant Cards

Students enjoy it when teachers "hype" things up to keep their attention. At the beginning of the school year, have each student print or write his or her name on a Contestant Card. After you collect them, laminate the cards and put them together with a rubber band or in a small box so that they make a deck of cards. You can use the cards to dole out privileges, such as choosing a supply clerk, or you can use them during discussion time as a way to keep students' attention by randomly calling on them for answers.

"Let's see now, who's the next contestant?"

 Tip:

Shuffle the cards often so students don't quit paying attention after their turn.

The Next Contestant Is:

The Next Contestant Is:

The Next Contestant Is:

The Next Contestant Is:

The Next Contestant Is:

The Next Contestant Is:

The Next Contestant Is:

The Next Contestant Is:

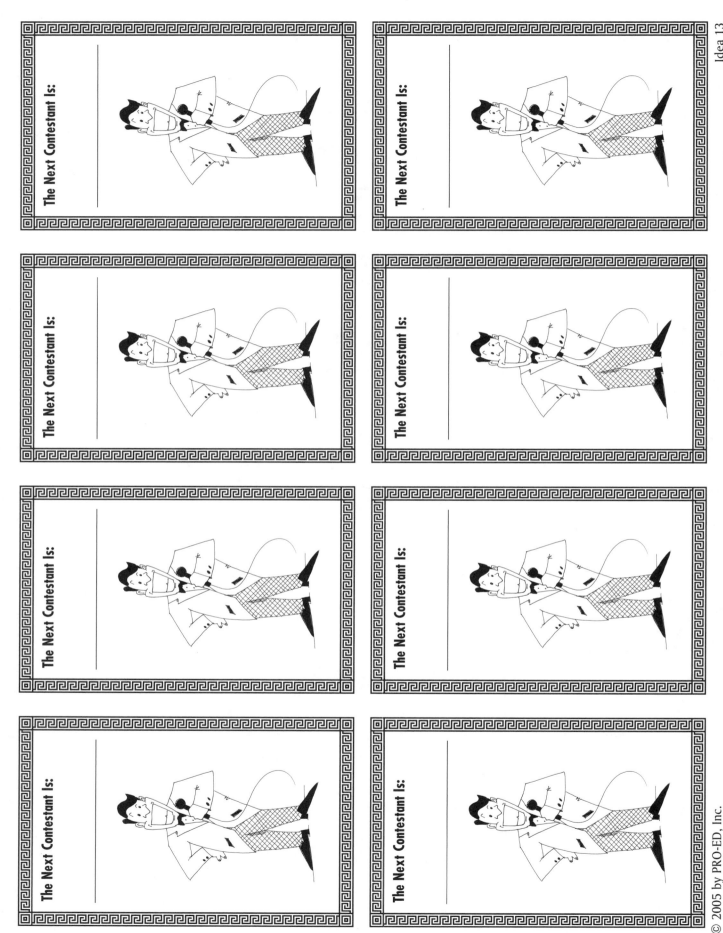

Idea 14
Self-Checklist

Help students remember their tasks and the order in which to do them. To create a self-checklist, write the tasks you want the student to accomplish on the lines. When each task is completed, the student puts a check in the star beside the task. Don't make the checklist too long, or students won't be able to keep track of things. Four or five items at a time are probably enough.

Did you do it?

Put a check in the star after you complete each task.

1 _____ ☆

2 _____ ☆

3 _____ ☆

4 _____ ☆

5 _____ ☆

Idea 14

Idea 15
Random Checks To Monitor Attention

You can do random checks several different ways, but the principle is the same: to monitor and reinforce students' attention to task at regular but unpredictable intervals. Remember to also check students at times when most of them are working hard and on-task. This gives them positive feedback and puts them on the road to success.

One way to implement this idea is to use a timer. Set the timer, but don't tell your students when it's going to go off. (You can face the timer toward a wall or window.) Everyone who is attending when the timer goes off gets a check mark in the Yes or On Task column. Each check mark earns 2 minutes of talk time, a raffle ticket, and so on.

Am I Working?

☑ Yes	☐ No
☑ Yes	☐ No
☑ Yes	☐ No
☐ Yes	☑ No
☐ Yes	☑ No
☑ Yes	☐ No
☑ Yes	☐ No
☑ Yes	☐ No
☑ Yes	☐ No
☐ Yes	☑ No

_7_ Yes out of 10

You can also create and use an audiotape that lasts for the class period. At random intervals record a sound such as a beep, chime, or gentle buzz. When the noise goes off, each student should ask himself or herself, "Am I working?" or "Am I on task or off task?" If the answer is yes, the student earns a class participation point. Points can be added to the classwork average or participation grade. The points can also be used as part of a contract system.

Note. Picture This was adapted from _Beyond Behavior Modification: A Cognitive–Behavioral Approach to Behavior Management in the School_ (3rd ed., p. 345), by J. S. Kaplan with J. Carter, 1995, Austin, TX: PRO-ED, Inc. Copyright 1995 by PRO-ED, Inc. Adapted with permission.

Am I Working?

☐ Yes		☐ No	
☐ Yes		☐ No	
☐ Yes		☐ No	
☐ Yes		☐ No	
☐ Yes		☐ No	
☐ Yes		☐ No	
☐ Yes		☐ No	
☐ Yes		☐ No	
☐ Yes		☐ No	
☐ Yes		☐ No	

_____

____ Yes out of 10

Idea 15

Picture This

On Task	Off Task		On Task	Off Task
		1	☐	☐
FIRST, I NEED TO MULTIPLY.	I HOPE THERE'S PIZZA FOR LUNCH	2	☐	☐
		3	☐	☐
		4	☐	☐
		5	☐	☐
		6	☐	☐
		7	☐	☐
		8	☐	☐
		9	☐	☐
I GUESS I NEED TO ASK FOR HELP.	FORGET THIS! I QUIT!	10	☐	☐
		11	☐	☐
		12	☐	☐

Total On Task = _____

Total Intervals = _____

Percentage On Task = _____

Idea 15

Idea 16

Three Bs

Teachers frequently find themselves wishing that students with ADHD would demonstrate self-control, especially when interacting with others. Actually teaching the self-control skills can be a challenge, however, because teachers have little time and few materials to provide them with ideas. Fortunately, there are some simple ways to teach self-control skills to students that require few materials at all. One example is the Three Bs. This is a cognitive–behavioral strategy. Teachers can teach a sequence in which students talk themselves through a situation without losing control.

Here's how to teach the Three Bs.

❶ Model for students by saying the steps aloud.

❷ Ask students to practice saying the steps aloud.

❸ Have students demonstrate the steps without actually talking.

❹ Set up scenarios or simulations, and ask students to demonstrate what they would do and how they would react.

❺ Provide students with corrective feedback and praise.

Three Bs

Be quiet
To calm down, stop talking.

Back away
To keep from getting more upset, back away.

Breathe deeply
Take one or two deep breaths to release stress.

 Tip:

Students can carry the small, wallet-size reminder card so that they can practice repeating the Three Bs throughout the day.

Three Bs

Be quiet
To calm down, stop talking.

Back away
To keep from getting more upset, back away.

Breathe deeply
Take one or two deep breaths to release stress.

Three Bs

Be quiet

Back away

Breathe deeply

Three Bs

Be quiet

Back away

Breathe deeply

Three Bs

Be quiet

Back away

Breathe deeply

Three Bs

Be quiet

Back away

Breathe deeply

Idea 16

Idea 17
Quiet Corner

All students can become fidgety and squirmy, but for those who consistently move a lot, create a special place where distractions are few and any disruptions are less likely to be seen or heard by other students. By careful observation and questioning, teachers may be able to determine which environmental conditions are best for individual students.

Here are some ideas for your quiet corner.

1 Keep the quiet corner away from traffic to and from the pencil sharpener, doorway, teacher's desk, bathroom, and water fountain.

2 Make the quiet corner a soothing (not a punishing) place. Do not use the quiet corner as a negative consequence or for punishment time-outs.

3 Remove posters and other distracting signs. Include some green plants. If you can paint, use a soothing, calm color on the walls.

4 For students who need formal furniture, use a study carrel that has sides and plenty of flat writing space. For students who need a more relaxed setting in which to calm down, use big pillows or a beanbag chair.

5 Identify the area with a sign like the one provided.

Quiet Corner

Idea 18
Provide Earplugs or Headphones

Large foam earplugs usually cost less than a dollar and are great tools for shutting out sounds. Each student can keep his or her earplugs in a plastic zipper baggie with his or her name on it and can use them during quiet reading or seatwork times.

Students also can use headphones. The headphones can be used just to screen out noise, or they can be attached to a radio or CD player that plays soothing, quiet music. Many students respond well to classical music with no lyrics.

Ordering Information for Earplugs and Headphones

World's Finest Ear Plugs
www.earplugsonline.com/index.html

Mack's Earplugs
www.macksearplugs.com

www.earplugs.gb.com

HeadRoom
http://headroom.headphone.com/layout.php

For reviews of headphones, see
www.headwize.com

Idea 19
Modify Movements

Students with ADHD are well known for some of their movements and motor habits. They tap, rap, tug, hum, twitch, snap, bob, and rock. We have provided some ideas to help students control these movements, which can distract themselves, other students, or the teacher.

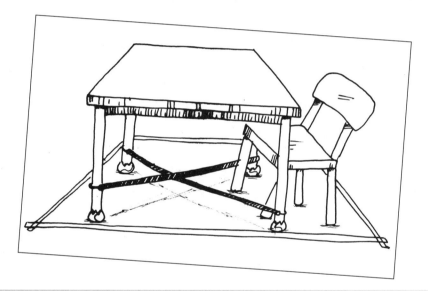

Try some of these.

❶ For students who tap, give them a mouse pad or some soft, thick shelf paper to use instead of their desktop.

❷ For students who are constantly touching something, give them a soft squeeze ball or some of the squishy novelty toys you can find at toy stores (gooey eyeballs, soft bracelets, etc.).

❸ For a student who likes to stand and move, use colored electrical tape to create a boundary around his or her desk. Allow enough room for the student to get up and move, but not enough space to bother other students.

❹ To keep chairs from scraping loudly, use tennis balls on the feet of the chairs. Just make a cross-shaped slice in each of four tennis balls and then slide a foot of the chair into each ball.

⬥❺ For the student who is always jiggling his or her feet and legs, take small elastic bungy cords and criss-cross them from the front right leg of the desk to the back left leg and from the front left leg to the back right leg. The student can bounce his or her feet on the bungy cords, which is much less noisy than tapping on the floor.

⬥❻ When you have a student who often finishes work early and needs to unwind, provide a Nerf basketball and a small hoop that attaches to a trash can or wall. Place the hoop at the back of the classroom and let the student earn 5 minutes of basketball time by correctly completing assignments.

Idea 20

Let Students Leave, But Make It Worthwhile To Stay

Students love to leave class to go to lockers, get a drink of water, or go to the restroom. When students get up and leave or ask to leave only occasionally, it does not disrupt instruction and is no problem. However, when students constantly ask to leave the room, it becomes a problem.

One solution is for you to allow them a certain number of "free" hall passes, such as our Get Out of Class Free cards. We suggest giving each student two cards per 6 weeks. Distribute them the first day of each new marking period after writing the students' names on them in ink (or you can have the students do it themselves). When a student wants to leave the room, he or she hands over a card. Only two trips are allowed for each marking period. However, for each card not used, the student can add points to his or her grade or test average or drop a homework grade.

Get Out of Class Free

This card is a hall pass for ___Polly Loehr___ who may use it for the bathroom, locker, drinking fountain, or _____.
_____

This card may be traded in at the end of the marking period

for ___2___ points on a test average.
___ points on a final average.
___ skipping one homework assignment.

Get Out of Class Free

This card is a hall pass for _____ who may use it for the bathroom, locker, drinking fountain, or _____ .

This card may be traded in at the end of the marking period

for _____ points on a test average.

_____ points on a final average.

_____ skipping one homework assignment.

Get Out of Class Free

This card is a hall pass for _____ who may use it for the bathroom, locker, drinking fountain, or _____ .

This card may be traded in at the end of the marking period

for _____ points on a test average.

_____ points on a final average.

_____ skipping one homework assignment.

Get Out of Class Free

This card is a hall pass for _____ who may use it for the bathroom, locker, drinking fountain, or _____ .

This card may be traded in at the end of the marking period

for _____ points on a test average.

_____ points on a final average.

_____ skipping one homework assignment.

Get Out of Class Free

This card is a hall pass for _____ who may use it for the bathroom, locker, drinking fountain, or _____ .

This card may be traded in at the end of the marking period

for _____ points on a test average.

_____ points on a final average.

_____ skipping one homework assignment.

Idea 21

Give Me Five

Some students with ADHD find it difficult to control themselves when they are frustrated, angry, or have hurt feelings. When students are in stressful or volatile situations that are likely to escalate quickly, it is often difficult to help them calm down.

Here is a simple calming strategy to teach students how to leave volatile situations. When using this or any similar strategy that requires students to use "self-talk," it is important to model both verbal and physical procedures and let students practice by talking aloud to themselves. When a real-life situation arises, they need to be able to talk themselves through it on their own. Visual reminders and cues are useful when teaching students to "Give Me Five."

Give Me Five

1 Stop talking → Count to 5
2 Take a deep breath → Count to 5
3 Let the breath out → Count to 5
4 Walk 5 steps away → Count to 5
5 Wait 5 minutes, walk back → Count to 5

Here are the Give Me Five steps.

❶ Discuss with students situations that cause them to be upset or angry, such as losing at a game, making a bad grade, getting reprimanded by a teacher, hearing someone call them a bad name, or asking for help and not getting it.

❷ Explain that one way to keep from losing control in these situations is to use the Give Me Five strategy and walk away from the potential confrontation or crisis.

❸ Model for students how to "Give Me Five." Demonstrate both the words of the steps and the physical actions. Here are the five key steps students should follow.
1. Stop talking. Count to 5.
2. Take a deep breath. Count to 5.
3. Let the breath out. Count to 5.
4. Walk 5 steps away from the person or situation. Count to 5.
5. Wait 5 minutes. If you're okay, walk back to the person or situation. Count to 5. If everyone is calm, begin to discuss the problem.

Note. Give Me Five is from *Practical Ideas That Really Work for Students with Disruptive, Defiant, or Difficult Behaviors, Preschool through Grade 4,* by K. McConnell, G. Ryser, and J. R. Patton, 2002, Austin, TX: PRO-ED, Inc. Copyright 2002 by PRO-ED, Inc. Reprinted with permission.

❹ To help students remember and to provide a cue of when to use these steps, use the hand gesture that indicates "Give Me Five" (hand up, palm facing the student, fingers clenched in a fist). As you demonstrate each step, raise a finger both to emphasize the step and to help students remember to count to 5.

❺ Next, ask your students to practice the Give Me Five steps. As they practice, have them say each step aloud. Let them use the Give Me Five cue cards if they need reminders.

❻ Review and practice the Give Me Five strategy at least once or twice a week. If possible, use a class discussion for students to share examples of situations in which they used the technique and how it worked for them. Make sure that each student has several Give Me Five cards to keep on the front of a notebook, in a wallet, on a desk, or in a pocket.

❼ Whenever you see a student starting to lose control, use the Give Me Five hand gesture as a signal to let him or her know that he or she should follow the five steps. Encourage students to signal each other if they see problems throughout the school.

Tip:

Students can carry the wallet-size reminder card so that they can practice Give Me Five throughout the day.

Give Me Five

1 Stop talking   →   Count to 5
2 Take a deep breath   →   Count to 5
3 Let the breath out   →   Count to 5
4 Walk 5 steps away   →   Count to 5
5 Wait 5 minutes, walk back   →   Count to 5

Give Me Five

1 Stop talking → Count to 5
2 Take a deep breath → Count to 5
3 Let the breath out → Count to 5
4 Walk 5 steps away → Count to 5
5 Wait 5 minutes, walk back → Count to 5

Give Me Five

1 Stop talking → Count to 5
2 Take a deep breath → Count to 5
3 Let the breath out → Count to 5
4 Walk 5 steps away → Count to 5
5 Wait 5 minutes, walk back → Count to 5

Give Me Five

1 Stop talking → Count to 5
2 Take a deep breath → Count to 5
3 Let the breath out → Count to 5
4 Walk 5 steps away → Count to 5
5 Wait 5 minutes, walk back → Count to 5

Give Me Five

1 Stop talking → Count to 5
2 Take a deep breath → Count to 5
3 Let the breath out → Count to 5
4 Walk 5 steps away → Count to 5
5 Wait 5 minutes, walk back → Count to 5

Give Me Five

1 Stop talking → Count to 5
2 Take a deep breath → Count to 5
3 Let the breath out → Count to 5
4 Walk 5 steps away → Count to 5
5 Wait 5 minutes, walk back → Count to 5

Give Me Five

1 Stop talking → Count to 5
2 Take a deep breath → Count to 5
3 Let the breath out → Count to 5
4 Walk 5 steps away → Count to 5
5 Wait 5 minutes, walk back → Count to 5

Idea 21

Idea 22
Self-Management

Many students who seem always "on the go" need some strategies for slowing down and relaxing. You may want to use these techniques at set times of the day with the whole class or with individual students using a cueing system. After you teach the techniques, play soft background music as the students practice.

Students who have difficulty focusing need strategies to help them pay attention. Visualization can help students "talk" to their subconscious about what they want to achieve or what results they want. Following are some techniques you can teach students to help them learn to relax and to visualize.

Relaxation

❶ Breathe in through your nose, counting slowly from 1 to 5; hold your breath, counting to 5 again; now, breathe out through your mouth, counting to 5.

❷ Focus all your attention at the tip of your nose. In your mind, watch the air flowing in and out. Count from 1 to 10 each time you breathe in and out.

❸ Visualize yourself stepping onto the top of an escalator. As you breathe slowly in and out, watch yourself descend into a deeper state of relaxation.

❹ Think of a peaceful place where you usually feel relaxed and happy, such as the park, the lake, or a favorite vacation spot. Picture yourself there, remembering all of the sights, smells, and tastes you experienced while there. Try to maintain a sense of well-being.

Repeat each technique for at least 3 to 5 minutes or until the student(s) feels completely relaxed.

Visualization

❶ Relax deeply using one of the relaxation techniques. Focus on a goal you would like to achieve. Picture yourself achieving the goal, including all the people involved in helping you reach the goal. Focus on positive feelings.

❷ Focus on a presentation you may be about to give. See yourself presenting your information in a clear, interesting way. See your audience understanding you. Focus on positive feelings.

❸ Focus on a problem situation. What do you want your end results to be? How do you want it to be resolved? Picture that happening with as much detail as possible. Bring all your senses into play. Picture positive interactions between you and the other person(s) involved.

Idea 23
Write a Contract

Students need support to reach their goals, and contracts specify precisely how a student will behave or what task the student will accomplish and in what time frame. They also specify what support a teacher, parent, administrator, or other person will provide to assist the student in meeting his or her goals. We have provided two contracts. The first is a three-way agreement, and the second is a homework contract.

Here's how to use the Three-Way Agreement.

❶ Meet with the student to discuss the target behavior or task.

❷ Collaborate to decide on the specific type of behavior the student will exhibit, the time span of the contract, and the specific support given to the student.

❸ Complete the form and have all parties sign.

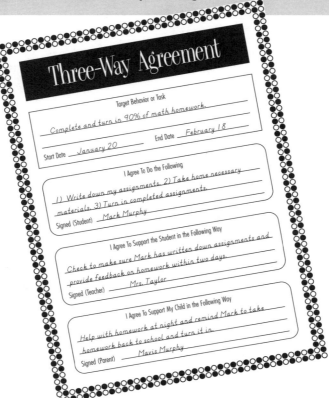

Three-Way Agreement

Target Behavior or Task

Complete and turn in 90% of math homework.

Start Date ___January 20___   End Date ___February 18___

I Agree To Do the Following

1) Write down my assignments. 2) Take home necessary materials. 3) Turn in completed assignments.

Signed (Student) ___Mark Murphy___

I Agree To Support the Student in the Following Way

Check to make sure Mark has written down assignments and provide feedback on homework within two days.

Signed (Teacher) ___Mrs. Taylor___

I Agree To Support My Child in the Following Way

Help with homework at night and remind Mark to take homework back to school and turn it in.

Signed (Parent) ___Mavis Murphy___

Here's how to use the Homework Contract.

❶ The parent and teacher create rewards that the child can earn for successfully completing and turning in homework. The parent provides a reward for completing homework, and the teacher provides a reward for turning in homework.

❷ The parent and child agree on the percentage of assignments the child must complete to be eligible for the reward.

❸ The student completes the contract with teacher input.

❹ The parent checks each assignmentl and circles Y if the child completed his or her assignment and N if he or she did not.

❺ The teacher checks to make sure the homework is turned in. The teacher circles Y if it is turned in, N if it is not, and NA if the assignment does not require work to be turned in.

 **Tip:**

You can use this contract for short- or long-term assignments.

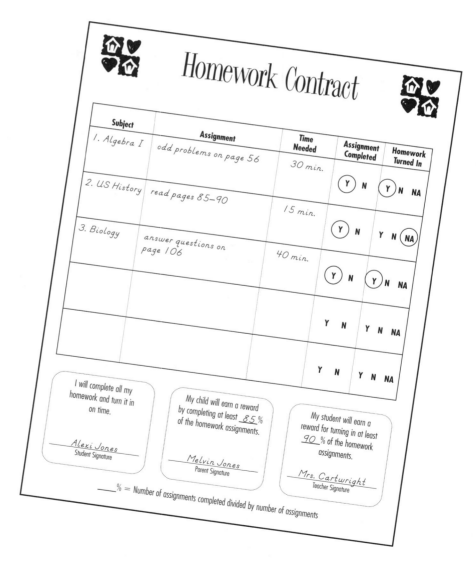

Homework Contract

Subject	Assignment	Time Needed	Assignment Completed	Homework Turned In
1. Algebra I	odd problems on page 56	30 min.	(Y) N	(Y) N NA
2. US History	read pages 85–90	15 min.	(Y) N	Y N (NA)
3. Biology	answer questions on page 106	40 min.	(Y) N	(Y) N NA
			Y N	Y N NA
			Y N	Y N NA

I will complete all my homework and turn it in on time.

Alexi Jones
Student Signature

My child will earn a reward by completing at least __85__% of the homework assignments.

Melvin Jones
Parent Signature

My student will earn a reward for turning in at least __90__% of the homework assignments.

Mrs. Cartwright
Teacher Signature

___% = Number of assignments completed divided by number of assignments

Three-Way Agreement

Target Behavior or Task

_____

_____

Start Date _____   End Date _____

I Agree To Do the Following

_____

_____

Signed (Student) _____

I Agree To Support the Student in the Following Way

_____

_____

Signed (Teacher) _____

I Agree To Support My Child in the Following Way

_____

_____

Signed (Parent) _____

Idea 23

Homework Contract

Subject	Assignment	Time Needed	Assignment Completed	Homework Turned In
			Y N	Y N NA
			Y N	Y N NA
			Y N	Y N NA
			Y N	Y N NA
			Y N	Y N NA

I will complete all my homework and turn it in on time.

_____
Student Signature

My child will earn a reward by completing at least _____% of the homework assignments.

_____
Parent Signature

My student will earn a reward for turning in at least _____% of the homework assignments.

_____
Teacher Signature

_____% = Number of assignments completed divided by number of assignments

Idea 23

Idea 24
Homework Forms

Getting homework completed and turned in can be a real pain for students, their parents, and their teachers. All students can benefit from tools that help them stay organized and on track with homework assignments. Four assignment forms are provided that can be used with students for varying purposes. Just having the forms is not enough, though. Teachers should teach students how to use them, let parents know what their role is in monitoring homework completion, and then reward students for using the forms regularly. For example, on the Long-Range Assignment Planner, the student, parent, and teacher initial each step that is completed on time. At the end of the assignment, if all the steps were completed on time, the student receives a reward.

Tip:

Parents will really appreciate these organizational tools, especially as their children get older and need to develop more independence.

Home/School Assignments

Subject	Assignments Due Tomorrow	Homework Due Today	Today's Classwork	Initials
_____ _____ _____	_____ _____	❏ Complete ❏ Not complete	❏ Complete ❏ Not complete	Teacher _____ Parent _____
_____ _____ _____	_____ _____	❏ Complete ❏ Not complete	❏ Complete ❏ Not complete	Teacher _____ Parent _____
_____ _____ _____	_____ _____	❏ Complete ❏ Not complete	❏ Complete ❏ Not complete	Teacher _____ Parent _____
_____ _____ _____	_____ _____	❏ Complete ❏ Not complete	❏ Complete ❏ Not complete	Teacher _____ Parent _____
_____ _____ _____	_____ _____	❏ Complete ❏ Not complete	❏ Complete ❏ Not complete	Teacher _____ Parent _____

Idea 24

Homework Plan

Fill in **What** the assignment is, **When** it is due, and **Who** and **What** you need for help.

☑ Put a check mark in the box after you complete each assignment.

	What	When	Who/What Can Help	When Complete ☑
Monday				☐
Tuesday				☐
Wednesday				☐
Thursday				☐
Friday				☐

Notes

- _____
- _____
- _____
- _____

- _____
- _____
- _____
- _____

Idea 24

Long-Range Assignment Planner

Assignment/Project _____

Due Date _____

PART 1 _____
Due Date _____
Teacher's Initials _____
Student's Initials _____
Parent's Initials _____

PART 2 _____
Due Date _____
Teacher's Initials _____
Student's Initials _____
Parent's Initials _____

PART 3 _____
Due Date _____
Teacher's Initials _____
Student's Initials _____
Parent's Initials _____

PART 4 _____
Due Date _____
Teacher's Initials _____
Student's Initials _____
Parent's Initials _____

PART 5 _____
Due Date _____
Teacher's Initials _____
Student's Initials _____
Parent's Initials _____

PART 6 _____
Due Date _____
Teacher's Initials _____
Student's Initials _____
Parent's Initials _____

Idea 24

Homework Planner

Date ___ / ___ / ___

Subject	Assignment	Completed
		○
		○
		○
		○
		○
		○
		○

Notes

- _____
- _____
- _____

- _____
- _____
- _____

Idea 24

Idea 25
Team Checkers

Students can team up to check and offer help to each other. This strategy can be a big time-saver for teachers. Distribute the Team Checker cards to students each morning and start the day with a peer check. Students check each other again at the end of the day. Older students can also follow up with a reminder telephone call in the evening. Students who complete their cards can put them in a jar for a raffle each Friday. The winning team can be rewarded with a No Homework Pass or some other special reward for two.

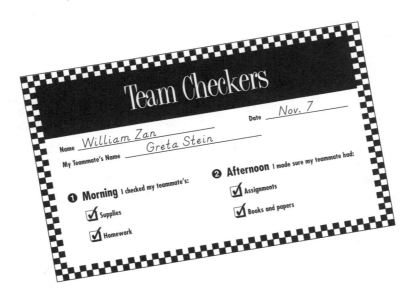

 **Tip:**

Switch partners frequently so that students get to know everyone in the class.

Team Checkers

Name _____   Date _____

My Teammate's Name _____

❶ Morning I checked my teammate's:

- ☐ Supplies
- ☐ Homework

❷ Afternoon I made sure my teammate had:

- ☐ Assignments
- ☐ Books and papers

Team Checkers

Name _____   Date _____

My Teammate's Name _____   Phone Number _____

❶ In the morning, I made sure my teammate:

- ☐ Had his or her supplies
- ☐ Brought his or her homework

❸ In the evening, I called my teammate to:

- ☐ Offer my help
- ☐ Remind him or her to do homework

❷ In the afternoon, I made sure my teammate:

- ☐ Wrote down the assignments
- ☐ Had the books and papers needed

Idea 25

Idea 26
Test-Taking Strategies

Students with ADHD can benefit from learning specific test-taking strategies. In this idea we present general test-taking strategies followed by specific strategies for a variety of types of test items. You can use this idea with small groups of students or as whole-group activities.

Here's how it works.

❶ Develop samples or use old test items, including directions. Item types should include multiple choice, matching, true–false, completion, and essay.

❷ Make an overhead or provide each student with individual copies of the test-taking strategies.

❸ Teach the strategies to the students using your sample items and directions as models.

❹ Practice one type of test item each week or day.

❺ Reinforce with practice items and discussion.

 **Tip:**

Use the coupons in Idea 27 to remind students of upcoming tests.

General Test-Taking Strategies

1. Always arrive early for the test.

2. Before reading anything on the test, jot down formulas and memory devices.

3. Read all directions underlining the important information.

4. If there is time, skim the entire test before responding to questions.

5. Answer easy questions first; save difficult ones for last.

6. Place a check in the margin next to skipped items or ones that need to be reviewed.

7. Identify and underline clue words in items. These include *never, always, usually.*

8. Review the entire test before turning it in to make sure that you have not mismarked the answer sheet or made some other simple mistake.

9. Review your old tests when studying for other exams or the final exam.

Idea 26

Strategies for Answering Multiple Choice Questions

1. Read the stem of the question and try to answer it. Then select the option that most closely matches your answer.

2. Underline or circle key words in both the question stem and the response choices.

3. Read all of the choices, even when the first or second choice looks correct.

4. Eliminate response choices you know are wrong.

5. If the response choice doesn't grammatically fit with the stem, it is probably not the correct answer.

6. If one response choice is all of the above and you know at least two response choices seem correct, then all of the above is probably correct.

7. If two response choices are opposite in meaning to each other, one of them is probably correct.

8. Always guess when there is no penalty for guessing and you can eliminate at least one option. Don't guess if you are penalized for guessing and if you have no basis for your choice.

9. Don't change your original answers unless you misread the question or if other information in the test indicates with certainty that your first choice is wrong.

Idea 26

Strategies for Answering Matching Questions

1. Read the question carefully before you begin matching items together. Make sure you understand what you are being asked to match.

2. Read each entry in the left column and try to think of the answer before reading the choices.

3. Read the column with longer choices first, because you will be able to scan the shorter choices quicker as you go through the questions.

4. Ask if you can use alternatives more than once.

5. Complete the answers you know are correct to narrow down the field.

6. Cross out each answer as you match it; this will help make it easier to see what choices you have left.

Strategies for Answering True-False Questions

1. Make sure that every part of the sentence is true. If any one part of the sentence is false, the whole sentence is false, even if there are some true parts.

2. Don't let negatives confuse you. If the sentence contains the words *no, not, cannot,* or other negative, drop the negative and read the remaining sentence. If the remaining sentence is true, the original statement is usually false.

3. Look for the words *sometimes, often, frequently, ordinarily,* and *generally* because they usually indicate true statements. The words *no, never, none, always, every, entirely,* and *only* usually indicate false statements.

4. When in doubt, guess true. You have more than 50% chance of being right with true (although this can vary from teacher to teacher).

Idea 26

Strategies for Answering Completion Questions

1. Underline the key words in the sentence.

2. Choose words carefully; the answer is often a technical word or important detail.

3. Read the entire item. If you think of more than one answer, write both answers in the margin, and when you go over the test later, choose the answer that seems most correct to you.

4. Check to make sure your answer fits logically and grammatically into the slot in the sentence.

5. Remember that not all completion answers are one word. If you can, consult with your teacher to see if he or she will tell you if the answer contains more than one word. If he or she will not tell you, use all the words that you think are necessary to complete the statement.

Idea 26

Strategies for Answering Essay Questions

1. Set up a time schedule to answer each question and to review and edit all questions. If some questions are worth more points, take that into account when setting up your schedule. When the time is up for one question, stop writing, leave space, and begin the next question. The incomplete answers can be completed during the review time.

2. Pay attention to how the question is phrased, that is, the words that are used. These include *compare, contrast, criticize,* and so on.

3. Outline your answer and sequence the order of your points.

4. State your main point in the first sentence and use your first paragraph to provide an overview of your essay. Discuss these main points in more detail in the rest of your essay.

5. Avoid definite statements.

6. Summarize in your last paragraph by restating your central idea and indicate why it is important.

7. Beef up your answers if you have time.

Idea 26

Idea 27
Date Reminders

Teachers often require students to take tests or quizzes home to show their parents. Unfortunately, this usually occurs after a student has failed or has not done well. We suggest that you take a more proactive approach. Provide reminders for students (and their parents) before a test or before a project is due.

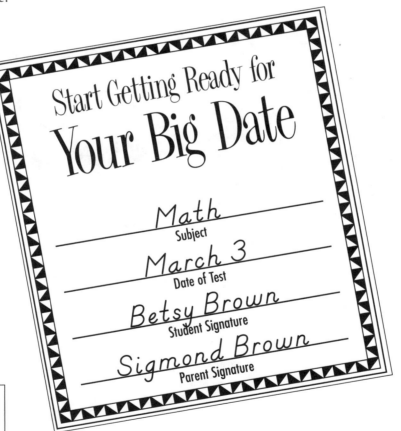

Start Getting Ready for
Your Big Date

Math
Subject

March 3
Date of Test

Betsy Brown
Student Signature

Sigmond Brown
Parent Signature

 Tip:

Copy the reminders on bright paper that is impossible to miss.

Don't Forget

On _____

☐ It's test time.
☐ It's time to turn in

_____

_____
Parent Signature

Don't Forget

On _____

☐ It's test time.
☐ It's time to turn in

_____

_____
Parent Signature

Don't Forget

On _____

☐ It's test time.
☐ It's time to turn in

_____

_____
Parent Signature

Don't Forget

On _____

☐ It's test time.
☐ It's time to turn in

_____

_____
Parent Signature

104

Idea 27

It's TEST TIME Again

_____
Subject

_____
Date of Test

_____
Student Signature

_____
Parent Signature

Start Getting Ready for Your Big Date

_____
Subject

_____
Date of Test

_____
Student Signature

_____
Parent Signature

It's TEST TIME Again

_____
Subject

_____
Date of Test

_____
Student Signature

_____
Parent Signature

Don't Forget Our Date for a Test

on _____

in _____

_____
Student Signature

_____
Parent Signature

Idea 27

Idea 28
Rewards for Neatness

Use coupons that let your students know you appreciate their neat work. Be specific about what it is they have to do to earn a coupon. After students receive coupons, have each one write his or her name on the back of it. Put the coupons in a large plastic jar. At the end of the day, reach into the jar and pick one. The student whose name is drawn gets a goodie (e.g., skipping a homework assignment, two extra points added to their test average, extra computer time).

Neatness Counts

This coupon recognizes your:

☑ Neat Handwriting ☐ Heading

☐ Complete Assignment ☑ Editing

Neatness Counts

This coupon recognizes your:

❑ Neat Handwriting   ❑ Heading

❑ Complete Assignment   ❑ Editing

Neatness Counts

This coupon recognizes your:

❑ Neat Handwriting   ❑ Heading

❑ Complete Assignment   ❑ Editing

Neatness Counts

This coupon recognizes your:

❑ Neat Handwriting   ❑ Heading

❑ Complete Assignment   ❑ Editing

Neatness Counts

This coupon recognizes your:

❑ Neat Handwriting   ❑ Heading

❑ Complete Assignment   ❑ Editing

Neatness Counts

This coupon recognizes your:

❑ Neat Handwriting   ❑ Heading

❑ Complete Assignment   ❑ Editing

Neatness Counts

This coupon recognizes your:

❑ Neat Handwriting   ❑ Heading

❑ Complete Assignment   ❑ Editing

Idea 28

Idea 29
Mnemonics

Here's a simple and commonly used acronym that can be adapted or expanded to help students check their work for neatness—"STOP." You can post this, then teach it to your students through recitation, repetition, and practice. Use the form as a cover sheet that students fill out and attach on top of each assignment. Also provided is a math problem-solving mnemonic, "FRED." It's fun to think of new strategies, so help your students generate mnemonics that work for them. We have provided two blank forms for you to use as you develop your own mnemonics.

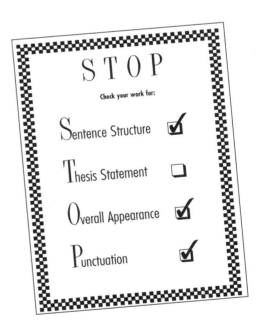

STOP

Check your work for:

Sentence Structure ☑

Thesis Statement ☐

Overall Appearance ☑

Punctuation ☑

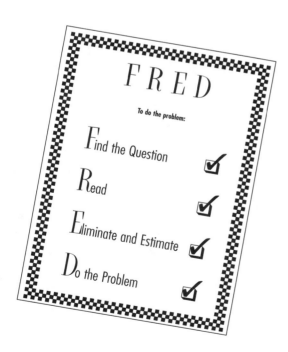

FRED

To do the problem:

Find the Question ☑

Read ☑

Eliminate and Estimate ☑

Do the Problem ☑

S T O P

Check your work for:

Sentence Structure ☐

Thesis Statement ☐

Overall Appearance ☐

Punctuation ☐

Idea 29

FRED

To do the problem:

Find the Question ☐

Read ☐

Eliminate and Estimate ☐

Do the Problem ☐

Idea 29

_____

_____

Idea 30
Boundaries

Provide boundaries for answers to questions or problems. Boundaries help students with ADHD focus on one question or problem at a time and help keep their work organized. You can use boxes, columns, dotted lines, or folds in the paper. An example is provided that you can use for almost any subject, including math problems.

Do Your Problems Here

Page __32__
Number __2__

$$6x = 12$$
$$\frac{6x}{6} = \frac{12}{6}$$
$$x = 2$$

Answer
$x = 2$

Page __32__
Number __4__

$$96 = 6x$$
$$\frac{96}{6} = \frac{6x}{6}$$
$$16 = x$$

Answer
$x = 16$

Page __32__
Number __6__

$$48 = 8y$$
$$\frac{48}{8} = \frac{8y}{8}$$
$$6 = y$$

Answer
$y = 6$

Page __33__
Number __8__

$$12y = 180$$
$$\frac{12y}{12} = \frac{180}{12}$$
$$y = 15$$

Answer
$y = 15$

Page _____
Number _____

Answer

Page _____
Number _____

Answer

Page _____
Number _____

Answer

Page _____
Number _____

Answer

Page _____
Number _____

Answer

Tip:

Use *Guideline Math Paper* for students who have great difficulty lining up math problems correctly.

Ordering Information
PRO-ED, Inc.
800/897-3202 • www.proedinc.com

Do Your Problems Here

Page _____	Page _____	Page _____
Number _____	Number _____	Number _____
Answer	Answer	Answer

Page _____	Page _____	Page _____
Number _____	Number _____	Number _____
Answer	Answer	Answer

Page _____	Page _____	Page _____
Number _____	Number _____	Number _____
Answer	Answer	Answer

Idea 30

Idea 31
Basic Graphic Organizers

All students can benefit from graphic organizers. By starting with basic graphic designs and teaching students how they work, teachers can provide a framework upon which students can expand as they progress through school. Some of the most common graphic organizers are presented here, along with simple directions for their use.

Here are the directions for the forms.

⊠ **Table It**

To organize information by category, topic, group, or characteristic, write or draw pictures of those headings across the top row. In the first column, list or draw pictures of the specific names or items being studied. Then fill in the boxes using pictures or words with the corresponding information.

⊠ **Let It Flow**

As you teach students a hierarchy in any content area, model the use of this structure by putting the influential or powerful item (e.g., person, position, or concept) in the large box at the top. Fill in the lower level boxes with pictures, words, or phrases, becoming more specific as you progress down the hierarchy.

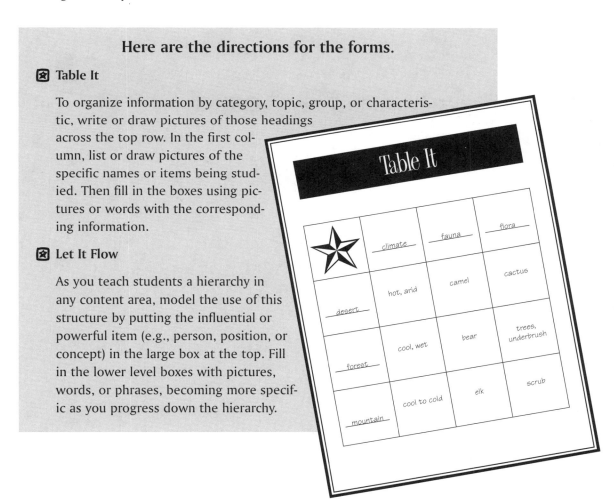

Table It

★	climate	fauna	flora
desert	hot, arid	camel	cactus
forest	cool, wet	bear	trees, underbrush
mountain	cool to cold	elk	scrub

Take Note

Teach students to use a 3-column format to take notes from their reading or from a direct instruction lesson. In the first column, have students write a concept, person's name, or word. In the second column, students should write the main points, definition, or explanation for the word written in the first column. Finally, in the third column, students should write some key words or a mnemonic or draw a picture to help them remember. To study for a test, students can fold their papers so that only one column at a time is visible. They should practice saying or writing the information from the other columns.

Spider

Use the spider to break a concept or theme into its major ideas and details of each major idea. Write the concept or theme in the middle circle, the major ideas on the rules extending from the circle, and the details on the rules extending from each major idea.

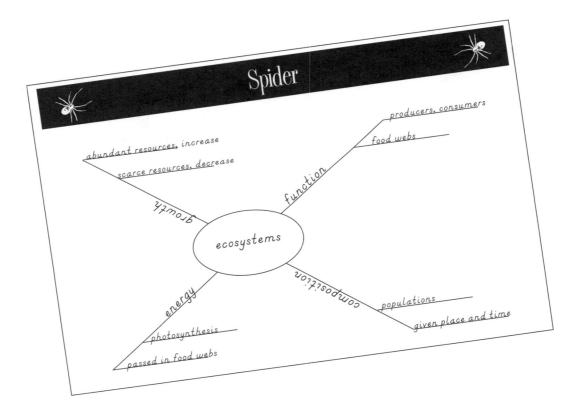

Table It

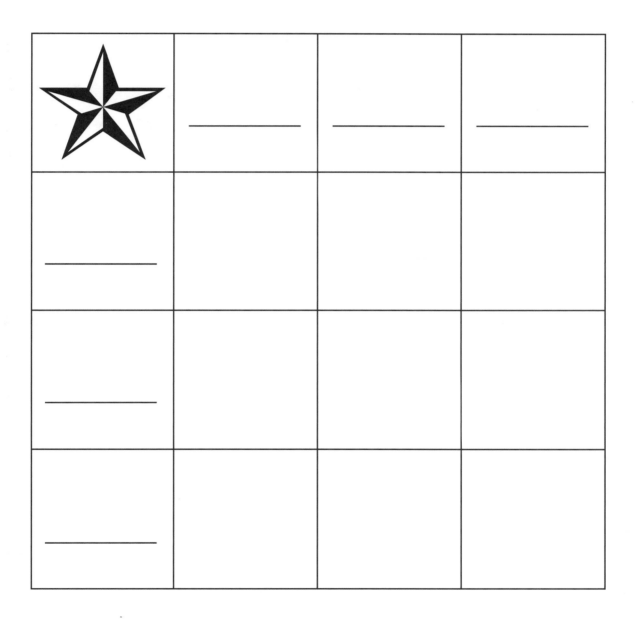

Idea 31

Let It Flow

Take Note

Concept, Name, or Word	Main Points, Definition, or Explanation	Key Words, Mnemonic, or Picture

Idea 31

Spider

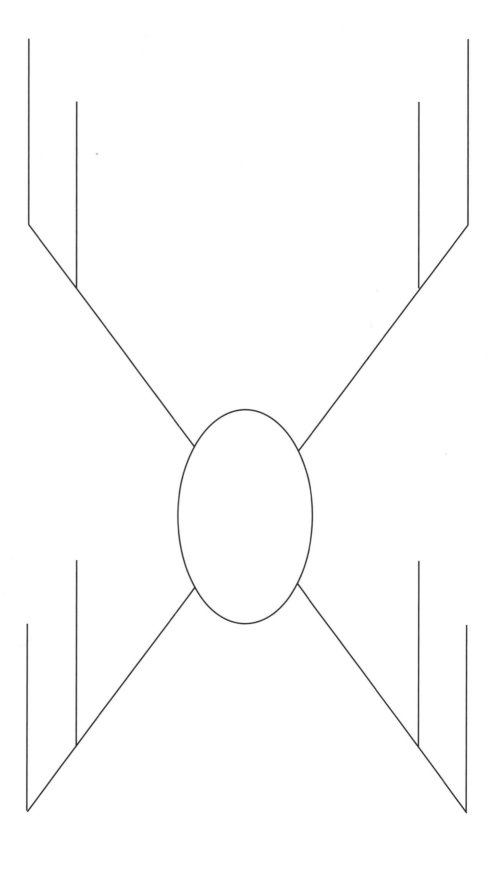

Idea 32

Cause/Effect and Sequencing Graphic Organizers

All students can learn to use organizers and structures that assist them with sequencing and comprehension when they read or after watching a video or DVD. Several graphic organizers are provided in this section that will help students:

• Understand what they read and hear

• Keep the information organized

• Learn about the main idea and sequencing

Here are the directions for the forms.

☒ Fishbone

Teach students to use this form to show the causal interaction of a complex event (e.g., the Civil Rights Movement, the explosion at the Chernobyl nuclear power plant). Write the result of a series of events at the head of the fishbone, the causes of the event on the slanted lines, and details that support each cause on the horizontal lines.

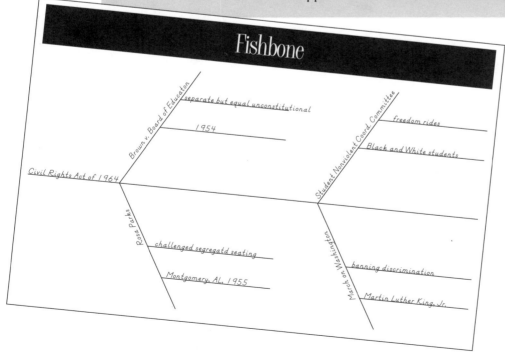

123

Story Chart

To demonstrate the use of this form, reproduce it on an overhead or enlarge it onto a chart tablet page. Read a story aloud, pausing to write or draw a picture of an important event in each box. Next time, have students write or draw events on their own forms, and then compare the students' forms to your completed form. Soon they should be able to fill in the form independently as they read or listen.

Sequence Circle

To help students retell a story or the sequence of events in a passage, teach them to write or draw those events on the Sequence Circle. This is a quick and easy tool that helps sudents see the sequence of events, the relationships among occurrences, and the causes and effects.

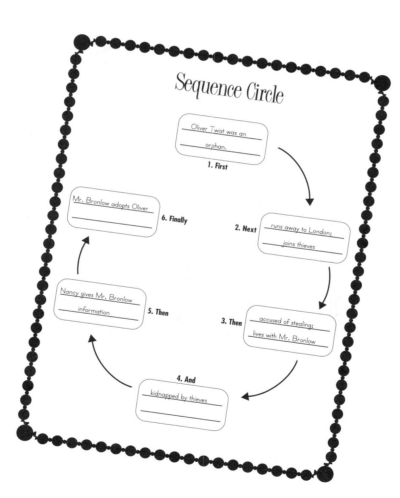

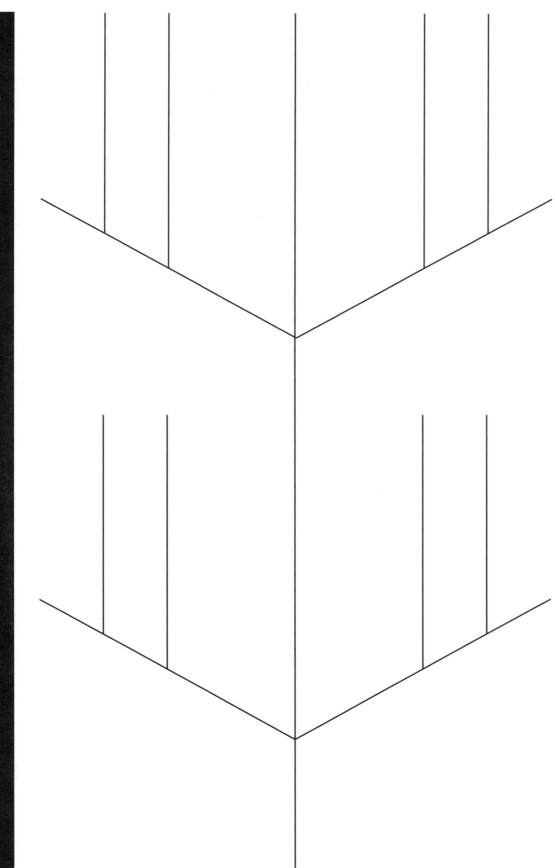

Fishbone

Story Chart

Fill in the events of the story as they happen.

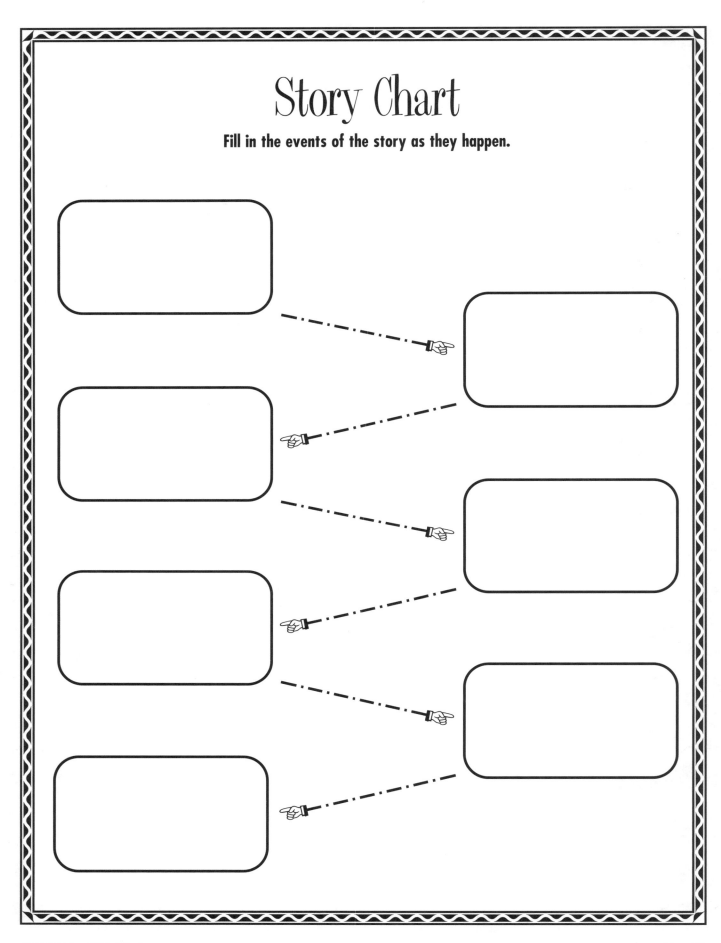

126

Sequence Circle

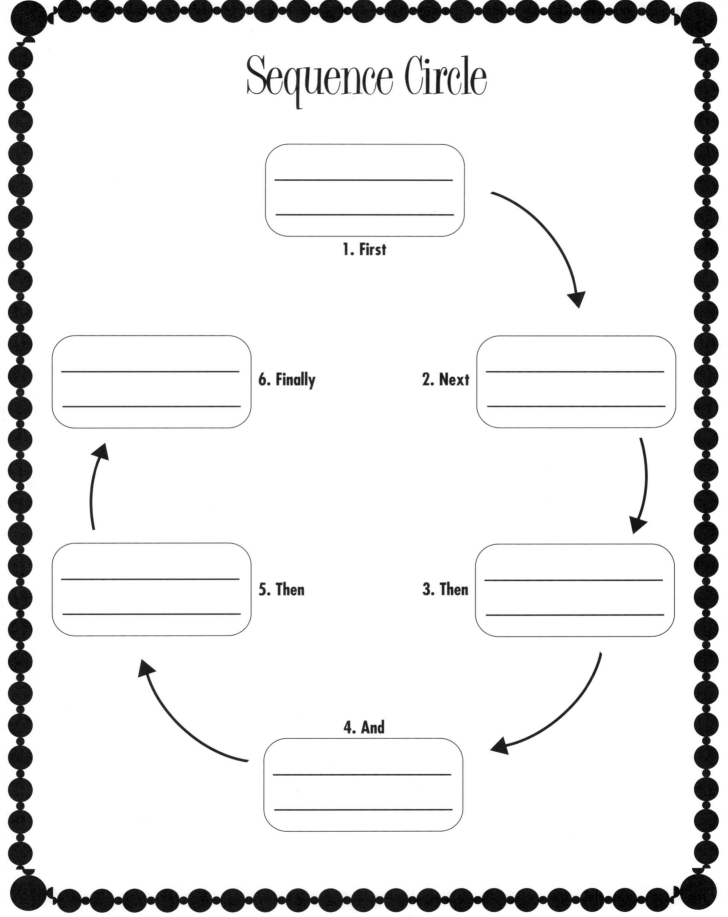

1. First

2. Next

3. Then

4. And

5. Then

6. Finally

Idea 32

Idea 33

Problem-Solver Graphic Organizers

Some strategies, such as graphic organizers, can help students take a step-by-step approach to solving problems and memorizing information. These organizers can be used to solve math problems, conduct science experiments, arrange historical events in chronological order, or complete any sequence of important facts. They can also be used to enhance creative problem solving.

Here are the directions for the forms.

⚝ Take These Steps

Take These Steps is a simple form to help students organize information. Have students write information or draw pictures in the boxes, and then use the form as a study guide by retracing the steps. This form is great for math problems and science experiments.

⚝ Web It

Many teachers use webs for instruction, to introduce topics, as a prewriting tool, to improve comprehension, and to explain relationships.

⚝ Synectics

Synectics was developed by W. J. Gordon in 1961. It is a technique to enhance creative thinking through using analogies or metaphors. It can be used for group work or individually to help students

- generate writing
- retain new information
- explore social problems
- define new words

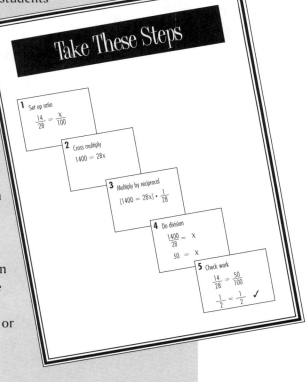

Take These Steps

1 Set up ratio

$$\frac{14}{28} = \frac{X}{100}$$

2 Cross multiply

$$1400 = 28x$$

3 Multiply by reciprocal

$$[1400 = 28x] \cdot \frac{1}{28}$$

4 Do division

$$\frac{1400}{28} = X$$

$$50 = X$$

5 Check work

$$\frac{14}{28} = \frac{50}{100}$$

$$\frac{1}{2} = \frac{1}{2} \checkmark$$

Here's how to use the synectics form.

❶ In the first column, students should make a direct analogy by finding a synonym to the word or theme.

❷ In the second column, students make personal analogie by describing what it would feel like to have this trait or characteristic. Have students describe their emotions or physical attributes here.

❸ The third column is for compressed conflicts. Students write an antonym to the word or theme.

❹ In the last column, students should synthesize the information by defining the word or theme (synthesis).

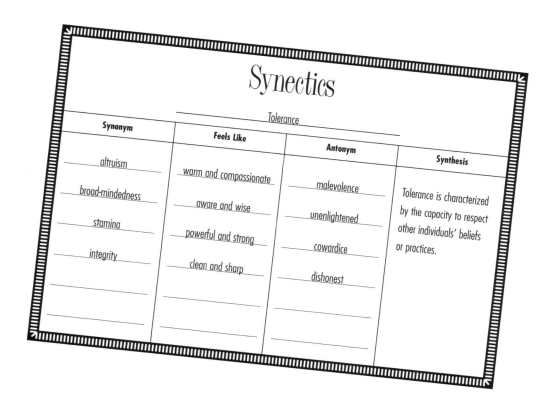

Synectics

Tolerance

Synonym	Feels Like	Antonym	Synthesis
altruism	warm and compassionate	malevolence	Tolerance is characterized by the capacity to respect other individuals' beliefs or practices.
broad-mindedness	aware and wise	unenlightened	
stamina	powerful and strong	cowardice	
integrity	clean and sharp	dishonest	

Take These Steps

Idea 33

Web It

Idea 33

Web It

Idea 33

Synectics

Synonym	Feels Like	Antonym	Synthesis

Idea 34
Compare-and-Contrast Graphic Organizers

All students benefit from learning the skills of comparing and contrasting. These skills help students as they categorize and eventually master concepts by determining whether items and ideas are the same or different. The three graphic organizers in this section should make it easier for students to compare things that are alike and to contrast things that are different.

Here are the directions for the forms.

✪ Same/Different

The Same/Different form is useful for students as they begin to differentiate and compare two ideas, objects, stories, events, characters, and so on. Students put the names of the two things to be compared at the top (for students who don't write, draw a picture or write the names for them); next they list or draw a picture of the characteristics or properties of the first thing that are different in the left column and characteristics or properties of the second thing in the right column; and finally they list or draw a picture of those characteristics the two things have in common in the middle column. Students can use their lists for discussion, writing, and study.

✪ Venn Diagram

Venn diagrams are commonly used in school, and students can be taught how to fill in the diagram even in very early grades. The Venn Diagram can be used in the same manner as the Same/Different form. The boundaries and visual representation should help many students who can fit their writing into the visual graphic, but may have trouble staying on the regular lines of notebook paper. Students who don't read or write can draw pictures or place manipulatives in the correct section.

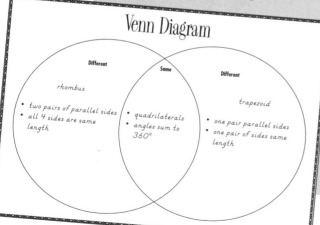

Attribute Listing

Attribute listing can be used to compare solutions to problems. To use the form, choose a problem and list several categories of the problem in the category column. In the attribute column, list one or more arributes of each category. Develop one or more ideas for improving the attribute in the third column. Write at least one positive feature and one negative feature of each idea for improvement in the last column.

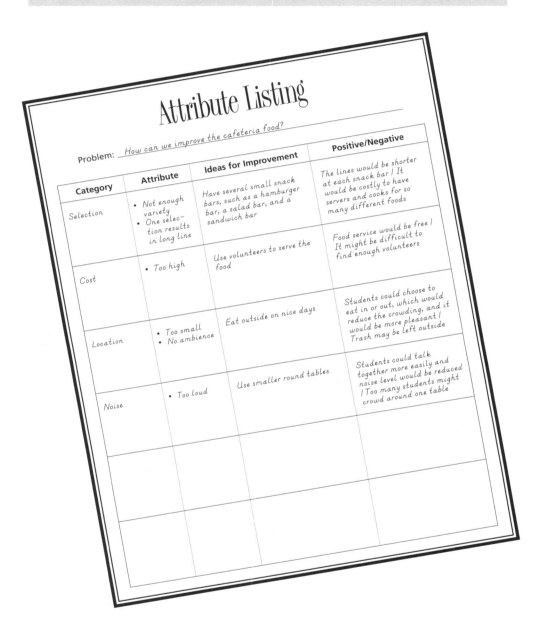

Attribute Listing

Problem: _How can we improve the cafeteria food?_

Category	Attribute	Ideas for Improvement	Positive/Negative
Selection	• Not enough variety • One selection results in long line	Have several small snack bars, such as a hamburger bar, a salad bar, and a sandwich bar	The lines would be shorter at each snack bar / It would be costly to have servers and cooks for so many different foods
Cost	• Too high	Use volunteers to serve the food	Food service would be free / It might be difficult to find enough volunteers
Location	• Too small • No ambience	Eat outside on nice days	Students could choose to eat in or out, which would reduce the crowding, and it would be more pleasant / Trash may be left outside
Noise	• Too loud	Use smaller round tables	Students could talk together more easily and noise level would be reduced / Too many students might crowd around one table

Note. Attribute Listing is from *Practical Ideas That Really Work for Students Who Are Gifted,* by G. Ryser and K. McConnell, 2003, Austin, TX: PRO-ED, Inc. Copyright 2003 by PRO-ED, Inc. Reprinted with permission. The Attribute Listing form was originally adapted from "Fostering Creative Thinking" (pp. 399–444), by B. Cramond, in F. A. Karnes and S. M. Bean (Eds.), *Methods and Materials for Teaching the Gifted,* 2001, Waco, TX: Prufrock Press. Copyright 2001 by Prufrock Press. Adapted with permission.

Same/Different

1		2		
_____		_____		

Different	Same	Different

Idea 34

Venn Diagram

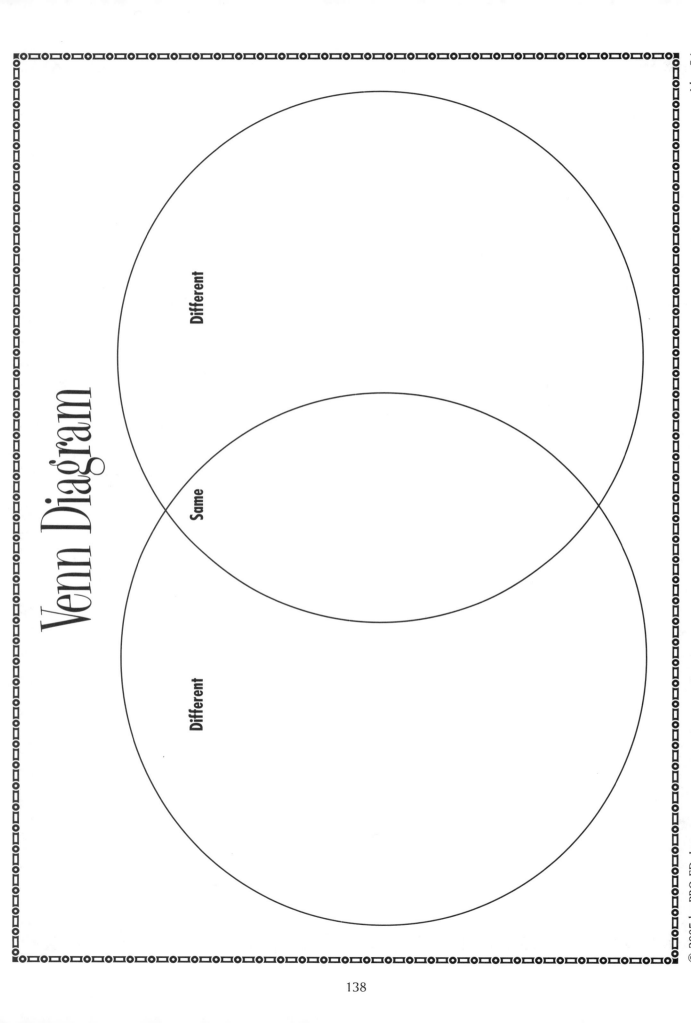

Different

Same

Different

Attribute Listing

Problem: _____

Category	Attribute	Ideas for Improvement	Positive/Negative

Idea 34

Idea 35
Post-it Notes

Outlining is difficult for students with ADHD because of their inability to focus. This idea uses Post-it Notes to teach students to make good outlines by recording one word notes and organizing them from the big ideas to specifics. To implement this idea you will need three or four different colors of Post-it Notes.

Here's how it works.

❶ Arrange students into small groups of three or four.

❷ Assign a passage to be read or give a short lecture. While reading or listening, group members write one-word notes on the Post-it Notes. Each note is given a level of 1 through 3 or 4. Level 1 notes are the big ideas, Level 2 notes get more specific, and so on. All words that have a similar relationship are given the same level.

❸ Organize the notes into an outline until all members of the group are satisfied. To organize the notes, group members should select the first big idea (Level 1) and place its related Level 2 and Level 3 notes under it. Then they choose the second big idea and place its related Level 2 and Level 3 notes under it, and so on.

❹ Complete this activity in one of the following ways, or come up with your own strategy.

- Use the outline master included so that group members can transfer their Post-it Note outline to keep for study purposes.

- Share the outlines with other groups, and develop a final class outline.

- Rotate groups among the outlines. Each group should make one change to make the outline better.

Outline

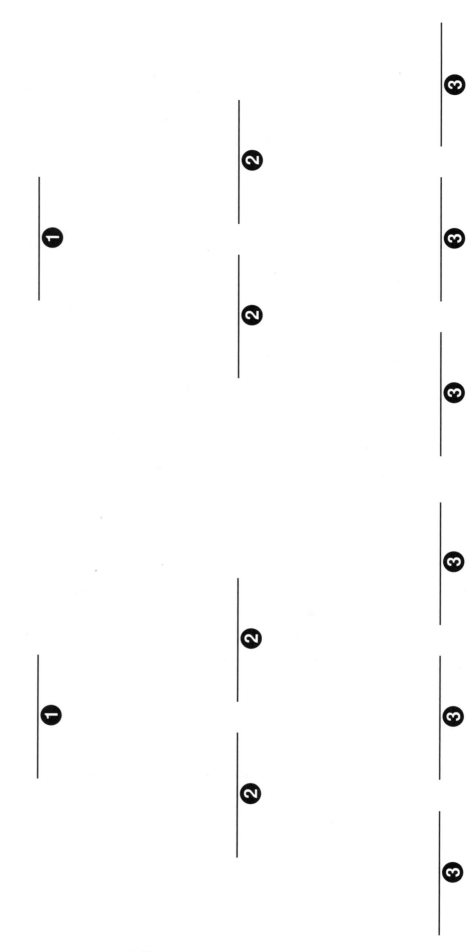

1 _____

1 _____

2 _____

2 _____

2 _____

2 _____

3 _____

3 _____

3 _____

3 _____

3 _____

3 _____

Idea 35

Idea 36
Not Just Underlining

Here's a variation on highlighting. This idea is especially helpful if your students don't have access to different colors of highlighters. All it takes is a pencil or a pen!

Here's how it works.

❶ Share the rules of Not Just Underlining (see next page) with your students, either by making an overhead or by writing them on chart paper.

❷ Make copies of a reading passage that contains all of the elements contained in the rules (i.e., main idea, key words, dates, references to figures, and important people).

❸ Give each student a copy of the reading passage and ask the students to read silently through the passage, marking it as they go along.

❹ Reread the passage together, calling on students to share their markings.

Tip:

- Give students a clear transparency to clip over a reading so that they can underline as they read the textbook.

- Teach students to put a box around the question words and two lines under key directions when taking tests.

Note. Not Just Underlining is from *Practical Ideas That Really Work for Students with Dyslexia, and Other Reading Disorders,* by J. Higgins, K. McConnell, J. R. Patton, and G. R. Ryser, 2003, Austin, TX: PRO-ED, Inc. Copyright 2003 by PRO-ED, Inc. Reprinted with permission.

Not Just Underlining

═══ Put two lines under the main idea.

▭ Draw a box around the key words.

⬭ Circle important people.

△ Place a triangle around dates.

∿ Make a squiggle under references to other information, such as charts, maps, or graphs.

Idea 36

Idea 37
Note Taking Made Easy

Taking notes is a skill with which many students with ADHD have difficulty. Teaching the art of note taking can be a frustrating experience for both teachers and students. Yet it is an important skill, particularly for students who are in middle and secondary school. We have included some of the most common methods one can use to enhance note taking and make it easier.

Cornell Method

The Cornell method was developed by Dr. Walter Pauk, a Cornell University professor, and is a method of organizing notes for effective studying.

 Use the Recall column to reduce recorded notes to include only the most important information from the lecture. Students write key words and phrases here.

 Use the Record column to record important information from the lecture. Students write key phrases, draw illustrations, make diagrams, and record questions and answers posed by the teacher here.

 Use the Summary row to summarize all the notes at the bottom of the page. Students will write one to three sentences that highlight the most important parts of the lecture.

(Allow students time to complete steps 2 and 3 immediately after the lecture.)

 Tip:

To review for a test, have students cover the Record column, leaving the Recall column exposed. Next, have students say each word or phrase out loud, then recall the information in the Record column. Finally, have students check how closely they match what they actually wrote in the Record column by removing the card. If they match, they should place a check by the word or phrase in the Recall column. If they don't match, they should star it as a reminder to come back to study it again.

Column It

This idea has forms to use to help students organize the information they read. In the left column of the form, the teacher or student writes the important headings (this column is already filled out in two of the forms provided). The headings provide guidance to the student to organize what they are reading. For example, students might use the language arts form when reading a short story. The first heading is setting and the student is to describe the setting in the right column. After students understand how these forms work, allow them to personalize the forms to fit their needs, with the format varying according to the subject area.

We have provided a form for language arts and a form for mathematics. There is also a blank form for students or teachers to personalize.

Symbol Shortcuts

Written language was not developed with an emphasis on speed, and usually the best speed of writing is about 35 words per minute. This makes notetaking even more difficult for students with ADHD. Use the Symbol Shortcuts page to teach students some common symbols they can use to speed up their writing. You can use Symbol Shortcuts in three different ways:

⌘ Enlarge Symbol Shortcuts and post it on the wall. Clip a pen to the poster for students to add their invented or suggested symbols.

⌘ Make an overhead of the Symbol Shortcuts page. Use it as a whole-class activity, adding students' invented or suggested symbols at the bottom.

⌘ Give each student a copy of the Symbol Shortcuts page to put in their notebooks. Allow them to personalize it by adding their own invented or suggested symbols.

Cornell Method

Class _____   **Date** _____

Topic _____

Recall	Record

Summary

Idea 37

Column It

Language Arts

Setting	
Characters	
Main Problem	
Goal	
Events	
Resolution	

Column It
Math

Main Idea	
Important Fact	
Clues	
Picture/Diagram	
Prediction	
Do the work and check.	

149

Idea 37

Column It

Symbol Shortcuts

Symbol	Meaning
=	equal to, same as
<	fewer or less than
>	more or greater than
*	important
w/	with
w/o	without
e.g.	for example
↑	increasing
↓	decreasing
≈	approximately
∴	therefore
+	and
i.e.	that is
b/c	because
Esp	especially
b/4	before
b/t	between
#	number
%	percent

Idea 37